Only by the
Grace of God

Only by the
Grace of God

*One Family's Story of Survival during World War II
as Prisoners of War in the Philippines*

Pamela J. Brink , Robert A. Brink, and John W. Brink

ARCHWAY
PUBLISHING

Archway Publishing books may be ordered through booksellers or by contacting:

Archway Publishing
1663 Liberty Drive
Bloomington, IN 47403
www.archwaypublishing.com
1 (888) 242-5904

ISBN: 978-1-4808-4070-6 (sc)
ISBN: 978-1-4808-4071-3 (e)

Library of Congress Control Number: 2016919830

Print information available on the last page.

Archway Publishing rev. date: 12/28/2016

Also by Pamela J. Brink

Brink, Pamela J., ed. *Transcultural Nursing: A Book of Readings*, Prentice-Hall, 1976. Reissued by Waveland Press, 1990.

With Marilynn J. Wood

Basic Steps in Planning Nursing Research: From Question to Proposal, Jones & Bartlett, 1988.

Advanced Design in Nursing Research, Sage, 1998.

Dedication

In loving gratitude to our parents, who protected us as best they could:
Myron Edgar Brink and Maude Elizabeth Rice Brink

To Mother's sister, Mabel F. Rice
and
Mother's mother, Jennie Doty Rice,
Who gave us a home, as well as financial and
emotional support when we needed it most,
and
To all our friends who shared these experiences with us

Contents

List of Illustrations

Preface—Pam

This is the story of one event in the life of one family—an event told by the three surviving children of that family. The event: the experience of being a prisoner of war under the Japanese, in the Philippines, during World War II. Each of us wrote a memoir. The events are the same, but the memories differ in detail. The significance of each event differed. Some things are detailed in one memoir that are absent or covered superficially in another. Other memories contradict each other, and there is no way now to clarify that incident. The memories have faded, perhaps distorted over the years, but the impact is still felt. No member of the family kept a journal or diary. There are some letters written before and after the war that the recipients saved and later sent back to us. They are included. Photographs sent to relatives are all that document a lifestyle before the war.

Our rescue from the Los Baños prison camp is well documented. It was an enormously successful strategic military operation preserved in books and on film and taught in military academies. For the internees, it was also enormously successful, as none lost their lives during the raid.

When we returned home, all that people wanted to hear about was atrocities. They were not interested in slow, deliberate starvation. Stories about civilian internees in the Pacific could not compete with Jewish stories of the horrors of the German Holocaust. Our stories were compared to theirs and were not horrific enough to hold anyone's attention. Our stories were ignored. The war in the Pacific had less meaning than the war with Germany. So we stopped sharing our experiences.

These memoirs have been written for the sake of historical documentation. They are the stories by the children caught up in that war.

None of us knew the other had written a memoir. Bill's was

discovered after his death. His are brief but probably the most accurate of the three. Bob's is full of detail, naming people I had forgotten. He was a gifted writer but could not participate in any revisions, as he died three months before Bill. I am the only one left to tell our story.

Bob wrote a good introduction to our family, who we were and how we came to be in the Philippines. I wrote another, slightly different, version of the family history.

Bill was the oldest child. He was thirteen when we were captured, so his memories are probably more accurate than either Bob's or mine. His memory of the day the soldiers came to our house and took our father prisoner, and the subsequent events leading to us eventually joining him in the city jail, are the gold standard of that experience. Bob and I have different versions, which are distorted by the eyes of fearful children.

Our stories are told in chronological order; the events are listed in a timeline by Bill. Each event is described: first Bill's notes, then Bob's, and then mine. I have appended letters and documents that validate our memories. I am grateful to those relatives who had saved our letters.

My version of these events is a child's story of a period in my childhood, and as such has all the inaccuracies and distortions of a child. If my brothers had ever read my version, they would have said "No! That's not at all what happened. You've got it wrong." I have found over the years that all of us have distorted memories. We tend to remember an event that had some personal meaning for us, and we only remember our perception or interpretation of the event, not the actual event itself.

Acknowledgment

I am unendingly grateful to Dorci Leara for her friendship and editing skills. Her constant support and patience throughout the development of the manuscript is gratefully acknowledged.

Bill's Timeline and Synopsis of the Major Events in Our Lives

1941   December 8—taken from school and evacuated to Montalongon

1942   April 20—Dad taken by Japs from Montalongon

        May 3—rest of us to Cebu prison

        May 16—left jail for junior college

        October 13—left junior college for Fillipino Country Club

        Dec 14—loaded on Jap freighter

        Dec 19—arrived Manila and Santo Thomas

1944   April 7—transferred to Los Baños

1945   Feb 23—rescued by Eleventh Airborne, Third Cavalry, and guerillas

Bang, clang, bang! Three shots through a galvanized iron roof. March of '42. Great way to wake a thirteen-year-old from an afternoon siesta. We looked out a window of our cabin in the mountains to see a company of Japanese approaching. We had watched their landing on the beach of southern Cebu two weeks earlier.

Braat, braat, braat! 6:55 a.m., February 23, 1945. We watched from a ditch as the Eleventh Airborne and Filipino guerillas stormed our prison camp. Some of us had watched them parachute out of their C-47s five minutes earlier. That was the morning we were to be machine-gunned at 7:00 a.m. roll call.

Three years we spent under Japanese rule. Many of us, Brits, Australians, White Russians, and Americans, (some who had passage home six months before Pearl Harbor) were still in the Philippines because the State Department was given instructions not to issue any exit visas. We might panic people into believing a war with Japan was imminent. Those who survived look back in wonder. We were just civilians. The military had it so much worse.

Chapter 1

IN THE BEGINNING

Bill's Description of Family Life Prewar

If a child such as I in 1940 had no referent for comparison, he would not realize that his life in prewar Cebu, Philippines, was not the norm. He was in for a rude surprise.

We—my father, mother, sister, brother, and I—were going home to the United States. My father had tickets purchased six months before December 7, 1941. We were not permitted to leave. I have that information direct from my father and later from Lucia B. Kidder (*Ex-POW Bulletin,* September 1990). See the letter of Maude Brink to her sister in September 1941, which stated that the family would not be returning to the States.

Bob's Description of Family Life Prewar

The Philippines are an archipelago lying in the South China Sea of the Pacific Ocean, southwest of Japan. There are approximately seventy-one hundred islands totaling the size of Arizona. The climate is tropical with abundant rainfall. The majority of Filipinos are of Malayan, Chinese, Spanish, Mestizo (a combination of Spanish and native islander), Negritos, Igarots, and Moros. Religion is predominately Roman Catholic. Language is mixed and is Filipino, mostly a dialect of Tagalog spoken in the northern part of the islands and Visayan spoken in the southern part. Pidgin English was used as a trade language when Spanish and English were not understood. Luzon is the largest island in the Philippines, and it has the capital, Manila. Cebu, a cigar-shaped island about three hundred miles south of Luzon, is where my brother, sister, and I were born. (I have been told that the most beautiful women in the Philippines, due to the combination of native and Spanish blood, come from Cebu.)

The Brinks, who are mainly of Dutch heritage, fought in both the War of 1812 and the Civil War. (Laurel Shanafelt Powell has written an extensive genealogy of the Brink family. See references.) My grandfather, John William Brink, was a South Dakota farmer and Protestant preacher who did not see the importance of college, much less the need for high school: he wanted farmhands. (See Stainbrook in references for information on the Brink family in Milltown, South Dakota.) My father, Myron, would have none of that. He was young and adventuresome and wanted, more than anything else, to get out of his native South Dakota. Myron, a redhead who disliked the name Red, was five feet nine and a half inches tall and weighed about 190. He had enormous forearms from milking cows. He was an intercollegiate boxer, a tennis player, a softball player, a scratch golfer, a horseman, and a fine polo player.

My father went to the Philippines at the age of twenty after putting himself and his sister Hazel through South Dakota Wesleyan University. (Bill Mattas, Hazel's son, says his mother graduated from college when she was sixty-four years old, so this doesn't seem accurate.) Dad took his final college exams in the Philippines and graduated Phi Beta Kappa.

He started out teaching high school math in a public school and found that teaching was not to his liking. He was much more interested in business. Dad resigned after the end of his first (and only) teaching year, and then he and two friends started a bank, with him assuming the role of secretary/treasurer. It didn't take long for the young entrepreneur to be recognized as a "go-getter," and he was soon hired by the Del Monte Corporation to revive a pineapple plantation at Cagayan on the island of Mindanao. Dad quickly and effortlessly brought that plantation to profitability. Again, someone noticed his inherent talents, and soon he assumed the position of assistant manager of the Philippine Refining Company. It was at that time that he met my mother.

Dad did not fight in World War I. He was, however, a captain in the Philippine Constabulary. Our house reflected some of his souvenirs. We had native *krises* (a manual-shot shotgun that required the pulling of the gun barrel toward you, where the firing pin was located), bows and arrows, and spears that had been taken from the Moros. The Moros were native tribesmen of Islamic faith who were always in rebellion against the constituted government. They are still in existence today. They lived on the island of Mindanao and, with their *dhoas*, preyed on shipping in the Sulu Sea. They had a quaint custom of ordaining a prince martyr who would have his body bound tightly with cord to keep the circulation slow and go *juramentado* (a mission to kill as many Christians as possible before he was killed).

The US Army's 30.06 rifle was not adequate to the task of subduing the Moros. The bullets would go right through them and were not lethal. The army had to invent the .45 caliber pistol to finally stop the natives running amok. The years before World War II were perilous times. Dad always kept loaded weapons close by.

My mother, Maude E. Rice, was born in Flintville and raised in Steven's Point, Wisconsin. Her ancestry is English, Scotch, Welsh, and Irish. One of our ancestors, Deacon Edmund Rice, came to America on the Mayflower (as an indentured servant). Another ancestor, Jeremiah Purdy, fought in the American Revolution. So mother qualified to belong to the Daughters of the American Revolution. Her father, Allan Dexter Rice, and two brothers, William and Allan, were lumberjacks working in the North Woods.

All of my mother's family members were tall. Uncle Bill was six feet four, Uncle Allan was six feet two, and Auntie Mabel was five feet twelve inches (as she liked to say in preference to six feet). My mother, Maude, was the same height as her future husband: five feet nine and a half inches. My grandmother Rice was a small woman with an iron will.

Mother and her sister, Mabel, attended normal school (a combination of high school and junior college) together. They put each other through school. One would teach the year the other was in school. Grandmother was the first woman in Wisconsin to receive a master's degree (from Columbia University) in mathematics. She taught high school, which began a proud profession of education in our family. After Mother graduated from the local Normal School, which included a two-year teachers' college, she taught eighth grade in West Alice, a suburb of Milwaukee. Her sister was her principal. Mother was a fine horsewoman and often rode with young cavalry officers.

Mabel Rice, my Auntie Mabel, was offered the position of assistant superintendent of schools in the Philippines at the request of the American ambassador, who had jurisdiction of the schools. At the time of the offer, Mabel had a boyfriend who had been gassed during World War I, and she did not want to leave him. She suggested that Maude go in her place. Mother jumped at the chance to leave Wisconsin and see the world. The job took her from island to island to inspect the US government-run schools. One summer, Mother took a walking tour through Igorot country and became, much to the relief of her family, the first white woman to survive. The Igorot people, who lived near the Cordillera administrative region in the Philippine island of Luzon, were headhunters and not much taller than the pygmy Negritos. Mother has pictures from her journal showing her towering over two little men in the forest.

Social life in the late 1920s centered around dinner parties, as most people went to restaurants infrequently. The parties gave everyone an opportunity to dine and, over cocktails (scotch and soda being a perennial favorite) socialize. Women wore long gowns, and men wore Walter Wither-designed suits or tuxedos. Maude and Myron associated with a small group of white people who were extremely biased. Gossip was rampant, and if anyone left the room, that person was fair game. Mother was asked to sing at parties until one of her closest friends said she didn't like Mother's voice. Of course, that closest friend soon discovered she was tone deaf.

Maude and Myron Brink with Leonard and
Rebecca (Billie) Self at a costume party

Mother and Dad met at the Army/Navy Club in Manila. Dad was
playing in a polo match there on his favorite horse, Lightfoot. After
a three-year whirlwind courtship, on February 29, 1927, my mother
asked my father if he would marry her. He stormed out of the room
while saying, "If I want to marry a woman, I will ask her myself." He
immediately came back into the room and asked her to marry him.

Mother had a diamond engagement ring that was the talk of the
islands. It was a two-carat solitaire mounted on a platinum ring. Mother
told us that Dad gave her a choice: an expensive honeymoon or a diamond
of her choice (and she could go as high as $1,000, which was a lot of

money in those days). Mother chose the diamond. A sea captain arrived in Cebu and carried diamonds for her consideration. No other woman in Mother and Dad's circle had a diamond of that quality or size. She wore a wedding ring, a diamond guard ring, and her engagement ring. Unfortunately, she only had her wedding ring at the end of the war. The engagement ring was hidden in Montalongon, and only our cook, Mary, knew where it was. She traded the ring toward the end of our captivity for some rice to keep us from starving to death.

Dad had, at one time, owned a rural movie house that caught fire one night. Because the movie house was made of nipa (a palm whose foliage was used for roofing thatch), the theater burned rapidly. Some of the moviegoers collected in the bathrooms, which were made of tin, and were subsequently burned to death. Their relatives wanted revenge and threatened to kill Dad. He began to keep a loaded pistol under his pillow until one night, soon after they were married, Dad woke up from a nightmare and knocked Mother unconscious. My mother also had kept her weapon of choice close at hand. She would hide a small dagger in her chest of drawers.

We were all born in the Southern Islands Hospital in Cebu City. (The hospital is still there to this day.) My doctor's name was Arlington Pond. I was born prematurely at seven months, and I only weighed four pounds two ounces. I was the second son, born eighteen months after my brother, John William (Bill). There had never been a Robert in the Brink family before I was born, and, in honor of Doctor Pond's ministrations, my middle name became Arlington. I now have two namesakes: Robert Arlington Brink II (I preferred that over Myron Edgar Junior—I never liked the name Junior) and his son, Robert Arlington Brink III. However, I have been told by my grandson that there will be no Robert Arlington Brink IV.

When I was born, we lived on the island of Mactan, near the city of Opon, in the Philippine Refinery compound. The Caucasian company employees lived there. We lived in the "big house," as was befitting the company manager. It was the first house to be seen when walking into the compound. A high mesh fence enclosed the compound, and we had watchmen patrolling the property day and night. The natives were not allowed in, and we, the kids, were not allowed out. There were no cars allowed in the compound.

We had a formal garden in front and a tennis court to our side. There were large trees covered with vines surrounding the house that Bill and I tried to swing on like Tarzan. The vines would always break. Our house had two stories with three bedrooms upstairs. A secret door in the closet of the master bedroom opened to the next one. I always wondered why. A large veranda completely surrounded the upper floor. Bill's and my bedroom was in the back. We were close enough to the ocean that we could hear the waves. The downstairs consisted of a living room, dining room, and bathrooms. The kitchen was a separate building that had a covered walkway between two buildings. I don't know where the servants slept. On the property was a small cave that had both stalactites and stalagmites and was home to hundreds of bats. We had a swimming pool, which Dad had installed himself. The main path branched out to the left and right of the big house to reach the houses of the other main employees.

Besides having some beautiful rugs that were made especially for the family in China, Mother and Dad collected antique Spanish furniture. They had an agent who watched out for the furniture coming on the market. The furniture was camagon made from red and black nara wood, a Philippine hardwood with beautiful grain, which was inlaid with ivory and pearl. The inlay was bent, not carved. (An art that has since disappeared.) The furniture was very old, and my parents would restore it. We had chairs, end tables, tea sets, and dining room tables of both red and black nara. After we were captured, ours were the first furniture and rugs to be loaded and shipped to Japan. We were very glad to hear that all that shipping was sunk. Today, Cebu craftsmen still try to imitate our lost furniture, but, unfortunately, the art of bending ivory has been lost

Visitors to Opon docked at the *pantalong* (a long wooden walkway from the shore ending at the wharf). The end of the pantalong had a roof built over the last part before we stepped down to the dock where Bill and I stored bamboo fishing poles and fished off the pier.

We were not encouraged to go to the beach because the natives used it for a toilet. Much to our parents' chagrin, Bill and I loved to play on the beach, especially when it was low tide. We could find all sorts of interesting animals there. We liked to pour soap in the octopus holes, force them out, and throw them at the girls. Once I found a sea horse in a tide pool and had it preserved in alcohol and brought it to school for show-and-tell. We would gather hermit crabs and use them for bait. We would light the end of a cigarette and put it against the shell; and when the crab scurried out, he went straight into the bait can. We always caught fish, although the *tomasockans,* or mudskippers, on the shore were too small to eat. The natives loved *guynimous*, their word for anchovies, with their rice at meals. The natives were very superstitious. They believed that if we hung our feet over the sides of the wharf, we could be dragged into the ocean by an *Ugoi* (a water sprite that lived underwater and loved to drown children). There were also the *Wok Woks*. These impish spirits played tricks and sometimes kidnapped and murdered foolhardy children.

The Padgetts lived in the next largest house, as was the custom of the assistant manager. Cy, or Cyrus, was a big, blustery man with a cigarette constantly in the corner of his mouth. When he wasn't sweating, he was flirting with anyone in a skirt. Cy's chubby wife was Blanche. Their son, John or "Jack," was a year older than Bill. Betty Jean was six months older than me. Betty loved to mother me, and when her family went to the States on vacation, I had to read by myself. Betty, Jack, Bill, and I were inseparable. All the other kids in the compound were too young for us to play with. Betty and I often took baths together until some of Blanche's girlfriends thought it was terrible that two five-year-olds bathed together. That was the end of that. One of my favorite stories was that Jack once got bit by a dog, and he promptly bit the dog back. It was the only fair thing to do.

The three mothers: *left to right*: Blanche Padgett with Jack,
Mary Cleland with Mary Lou, and Maude Brink with Bill

One day, Bill and Jack were walking ahead of Dad and Uncle Cy
and had this conversation:

Jack: "My Dad is the best golfer."

Bill: "No mine is. He has all those trophies that he has
won in the glass case at the country club."

Jack: "Well my dad is the best fisherman."

Bill: "No he isn't. My dad caught the most fish on our
last fishing trip. Remember he caught the shark."

Jack: "Well, my dad is the company manager."

Bill: "No he isn't. My dad is the manager, and your dad
is only the assistant manager."

Jack: "Well, my Dad is older."

Which left Bill with nothing more to say.

Gene, an engineer, and his wife, Pansy McAdams, who enjoyed wearing pith helmets at every opportunity, lived next to the Padgetts. They had an older son named "Junior." Junior could swim the entire pool length underwater on one breath of air. He also liked to impress the ladies by holding live cockroaches in his mouth while their legs wiggled out. Their house had a large brass door knocker that was shaped like a bulldog's head. Visitors would press his tongue to ring the bell.

The Pipes lived on the other side of our house. Freer Pipe was British and was the company's accountant. He smoked a pipe, so the Filipinos called him *Quako*, which means pipe in Visayan. He was tall, slender, and fair-haired. Mimi, his wife, was from Macao. She was petite, dark-haired, and very pretty, which caused much jealousy among the older women. They had a son, Teddy, and a daughter, Teresa, who were much younger than we were and, therefore, were not part of our group.

Lastly, there were the Richards. I do not remember their father. Their mother, Molly Batterton, had two sons: Branny and Teddy. They, as the British wont, were educated in England from the time they were eight years old, and we only saw them on summer vacations. They were a lot older than we were but were very nice to us younger kids. Branny eventually graduated from the British Military Academy at Sandhurst. He was captured at Dunkirk and was killed escaping, for the second time, from a German POW camp. Teddy was shot down and killed during the Battle of Britain.

Mother's social circle: *left to right*: Tess Landon, Reatha Parrott, Pansy McAdam, Maude Brink, Claire Wislizenus, Harriet Richards, Mary Cleland, and an unidentified friend

One house in the compound was always vacant—it was right next to the gate leading to the city of Opon. We kids loved to play in it. The windows were tiny and made from some sort of silica, and we could push our fingers through the panes. It also had a dumbwaiter that provided endless hours of fun. I once fell off the second-floor balcony when we were playing hide-and-seek. I tried to go from one outside window to another, lost my footing and fell to the rocks below. I scared myself to death but only got a couple of scratches. A lot of Filipinos came to my aid and hurried me home, where I was properly chastised by my mother, who used the phrase that kids fear the most: "Wait till your father comes home."

Mr. Vaughn was an employee who did not live in our compound. My feeling is that he was an engineer. He was a quiet and unassuming man, who always was referred to as Mr. Vaughn. He was the only black American I knew at the time.

Sacchi was the company's electrician and did not live in our compound either. He was, however, always on call when we needed his services. He and Simone put up the windmill at our Montalongon home. He was a small, dark man and skilled in his craft.

Simone was the company limousine driver and chauffeured all of our cars. He was a large, moon-faced, and pleasant man. He was good with children and never seemed to lose his temper. Although I never knew if he was a mechanic, the seven-man Packard always seemed to run like a top. We never saw him change a tire. He came with the company car, and when we moved to Cebu, he decided to stay in Opon. We never had a chauffeur again.

Go Go was the company nurse and gave the worst shots in the world. It seemed I never ever got a sharp needle. When the dog and I both had to get our rabies shots, we both hid under the dining room table. It didn't do us any good. Go Go's office was at the refinery. He was a nice Filipino man and had a good bedside manner, but I didn't think too highly of his medical knowledge. Unfortunately, he was all we had on Opon. He kept a mean gaggle of geese. When we visited him, they would charge us with their wings flapping and hiss like cats. Those geese were scarier than a pack of dogs.

Sheba (or Cheba) was the company's gardener. He was Japanese, had a raw sore where his nose should have been, and professed not to understand English. He would just grin and nod when we talked to him. He never seemed to work very hard and was always watching us. After we were captured and locked up at the Cebu Provincial Jail, he came by to gloat over our reversed positions. He was actually a major in the Japanese Secret Service and had been spying on us for years.

The only other American that lived on Mactan was Dad Cleland. His granddaughters were our age: Mary Lou, Marjorie, and Maureen. We called them all Mousy or Muggins Mouse. Dad Cleland owned a boatyard that was mentioned in the book (and later the John Wayne movie) *They Were Expendable*. He was a crusty old guy, had a huge old Colt .45, and could take his teeth out. (We never could figure out how he did that.) He was captured by the Japanese and tortured before he eventually joined us at Santo Tomas.

The three fathers: *left to right*: Myron Brink with Bill, Morrie
Cleland with Mary Lou, and Cy Padgett with Jack

The company had a small tugboat that we kids used for fishing.
The cabin housed the wheel and engine room, with a small overhang
on the aft deck to protect the outside galley. We would either sleep in
the cabin or on deck. We would catch red snapper, barracuda, *mumpsa*,
rumpy con dado, and sea bass. Flying fish would often try to leap over
the tug at night, and we always had some on the deck in the morning.
Dad always caught wheelbarrow loads of fish, and we woke up to flying
fish for breakfast. We usually returned from our trips tired and happily
sunburned. The tug is where I first learned to love the smell of coffee. I
never liked tea quite as much. Freer Pipe went with us on occasion but
was not a very good fisherman. One time we were outside of a sea cave
on the Island of Chocolate, and he decided to swim. He jumped over
the side and proceeded to swim into the cave, where he could see a lot of
deadly sea snakes swimming in the crystal clear water. Needless to say,
he was quickly back onboard.

Tanguingi fish on left. Barracuda on right.

When I was six, I was given a horse for my birthday. He was a roan stallion that I named Prince; he came from our cattle ranch at Bohol. He was a very tired little Filipino pony when I got him. After we fattened him up some, he showed us that he had a few tricks up his sleeve. He did not want to carry two people at a time no matter what size they were, so he would try to kick the second person, or he would inflate his stomach when he was being saddled so that the girth would slip. There were a couple of times when I found the saddle slowly creeping toward his belly. In the mornings, his regimen would fall into two categories: bucking us off or stepping on our toes. Prince was absolutely petrified of the whip. If I showed him any kind of a stick, he would bolt. He also liked to bite, and had a tendency to fight other stallions. I had him until the war. I was the only kid with a horse. Bill never liked horses, and Pam couldn't care less.

My first ten years were the easiest. The Philippines were a virtual paradise, and living was easy if you had money. We didn't want for anything. We had a large house, a nice car, good tailored clothes, plenty to eat, and many servants. We all had *amahs,* nursemaids as they were called in the Orient, and Bill and I had a manservant, Raphael, who was the brother of Mary Tumalok, our cook, and Ebing, our amah. We had *lavenderas*, or washing women, who would do all of our laundry and ironing. They used charcoal irons, and sometime the charcoal they used was extremely pungent. Sixto was our houseboy. We also had a German Shepherd watchdog, Guapa.

Dad with Guapa, the German Shepherd puppy
he gave Mother for a wedding present

My brother, Bill, reminds me that life was so easy that we never learned to put things away. I didn't even know how to tie my own shoes because I always had someone around who would tie them for me. When we got up in the morning, our shoes were always shined, our clothes were laid out, and, after we brushed our own teeth, our shower was drawn. After we were done, our valet was holding a towel, dried us off, and then helped us dress, including putting on our socks and shoes. In the evening, Raphael helped us dress for bed. I never had to go near a chest of drawers or a closet for my clothes.

Mother had a sewing machine that all the other mothers raved about, which she used to sew our undershirts to our undershorts so that our shirttails never pulled out.

Occasionally a large US warship would enter the harbor between Mactan and Cebu, where the *Morro Castle* sat. Dad would often go aboard, and we were allowed to tag along. These ships were much, much larger than our interisland sea liner, *Mount Mayon*, that transported people from Cebu to Manila and other islands. Once Dad took a business trip aboard a Ford trimotor airplane. That was a memorable occasion because we got to meet him at the airport where our three US Army biplanes were hangared.

Sometimes we were taken to the city of Opon. Mactan Island is the place where Ferdinand Magellan was killed by the native chief Lapu Lapu. There is a monument there to commemorate this event. On market day in the City of Opon, we would go with the servants and tour the market. There we could get fried bananas, bananas rolled in brown sugar, and ice treats; and, sometimes, we would get Bud Bud (a sweetened sticky rice steamed in banana leaves). Mary, our cook, always boiled rice with a banana leaf on the bottom of the pan, which horrified my mother.

The refinery was an interesting place. Natives would float rafts of coconuts, sometimes numbering in the hundreds, to the plant for processing. There the coconuts would be unhusked, broken in half, and laid out in beds open to the sun. The dried coconut meat, or copra, would then be ground into cakes, squeezed dry, and the resulting oil stored. Coconut oil had many usages, especially in soap. Dad once cornered the

Philippine market in coconut oil. He was always experimenting with the uses of coconut oil. He once even tried to use coconut oil as a substitute for kerosene. It never worked, and would have been too expensive.

We kids were not very interested in food as we grew up. Nobody had refrigerators. We had iceboxes that would use large blocks of ice to keep our food lukewarm. We sometimes snuck in with an ice pick to break off a chunk to suck on. Mother and Dad used ice chunks for their highballs in the afternoon. We had to drink powdered milk because we could not keep milk (or ice cream, for that matter) cold enough to keep from spoiling. Candy bars would melt in our hands before we got them into our mouths. Tobacco had to be kept in tins to keep out the mildew. Mother and Dad smoked Chesterfields because they came in round tins.

Everybody had a siesta after lunch. If we did not go to sleep, we had to be very quiet (this included the servants as well). After our siesta, we could get up and play or do our homework, but we had to be washed up and be presentable for 4:00 p.m. teatime. I never grew very fond of tea. I usually had mine with condensed milk and sugar just to cover up the taste. The British served high tea with scones (little cakes) and sandwiches. Americans sometimes served candy and nuts (we normally had nuts). Mom and Dad were not too crazy about candy. Dad had worked in a candy factory when he was young; and they let him eat all the candy he wanted, and he had never liked candy since. We usually had dinner at 6:00 p.m. We ate at the children's table until our table manners were good enough to dine with the adults. After dinner, we could read or study, or, in our case, Bill and I would build balsa wood model airplanes.

In the Philippines, it rained all the time—once a day in the dry season and all the time in the monsoon season. We also had typhoons, which meant heavy rain and strong winds. The natives had to tie their nipa huts down, or they would just sail away in the wind. Bill and I loved the heavy rains. We would strip off our clothes and play outside in the pouring rain while our folks were not around (much to the dismay of the servants—who always told on us).

We had the usual childhood illnesses. Bill usually brought them home from school. We all had whooping cough but skipped the mumps.

I had dengue fever. Bill had appendicitis and subsequent surgery and was not allowed to run for a year. German measles really made me sick. We had to go down to Cebu because Pam became delirious and almost died. We had our tonsils and adenoids removed. Pam climbed my guava tree and fell off and broke her arm. Somehow I got blamed for that. My horse was always trying to step on my toes if I was barefoot. He usually got him a kick in the slats for his trouble. I eventually got the mumps later on in life: My oldest son brought them home, and his brother, sister, and I all shared our misery. My wife, Barbara, had already had them, so I got to take care of everyone while she went to school. My brother, Bill, got them one summer in Blythe and was flat on his back for two weeks. Luckily, he had his lady principal to nurse him back to health.

We had German Shepherd dogs. They were intelligent, good with children, and excellent watchdogs. I learned how to walk pulling myself up on our dog, Guapa. She was also instrumental in teaching me how to swim. Dad threw us both in the pool at the same time. There's nothing like the possibility of drowning as a motivator. Dad usually had to shoot the dogs because they contracted rabies before they died of old age. We also had cats—*lots* of cats. At one time, we had fifteen. Pam had been given one cat, and that's how we eventually wound up with fifteen. My favorite was Kitty Gray. At the Boromeo house, a stray dog would come into the yard, and we would watch him nose around. There were cats hiding behind every pillar and post. On a given signal, the cats would charge the dog, and he would exit the yard with at least one cat clawing his back. We also had a cat name Bandit who had a stub tail. We took her up to Montalongon with us one summer. When it came time to leave, we could not find her. The next summer when we came back, who should come scratching at our door but Bandit, none the worse for wear.

Dad had a monkey when he and mother were first married. My dad's friends liked to get him drunk, and he would hang by his chain just out of reach of the dog, which would have made short work of him. Sometimes he would tear through the house, if he was loose, and wreak havoc until he came to Mother's dresser. He was endlessly fascinated by the monkey in the mirror. He would sometimes climb one of the trees, and the only way we could get him down was by Dad fawning over Mother. Then he would come down jealously chattering away.

We were never bothered by thieves on Opon thanks to the watchman that the company employed. When we were living in Cebu, there was an attempted robbery during siesta time. In the Boromeo house, we had a circular driveway planted with Singapore ground orchids, and robbers would attempt to steal them during the night. Dad would stay up with a loaded shotgun waiting for them. Mother always kept the pantry locked and doled out our rations for each meal to the servants. Otherwise, the food would leave from the back door as fast as it came in from the front.

Our cabin at Montalongon, a small enclave of mountain huts, had its share of robbers. Thursday was market day, and robbers usually tried to get in that night. They always got caught. I remember once when a robber tried to get in, and one of our maids cornered him with a shovel. Dad was in the city, so Bill wielded the shotgun until the robber was tied to the tree until the local sheriff could take him away. The sheriff, being a kind but naïve man, let the robber stay at his house before he took him to jail, where he promptly stole the family's money and chocolate and then ran into the night. The sheriff had the audacity, the *stupid* audacity, to show up at our house the next day and complain that we should have kept the robber tied up.

The Boromeo house was just across the street from a two-story monastery and right across the street from a convent. We went to Mass at the monastery, and many of the priests were close friends of Dad's, especially the Irish priests. We used to have them over for Christmas and New Year's. The convent would not let boys inside, but Pam was taught how to play the piano there. The monastery had a tin roof, and that alone was enough of a challenge for two little boys with slingshots. The best slingshots are made from guava tree wood. The tin roof made a definitive "clang" when hit. The best time to bombard the roof was during siesta time. The priests were sluggish then. We would hit the tin roof with a rock and wait to see who would come out. Just as the priest went back in, we would bombard the roof again. They finally figured out who was doing the shooting. We got paddled a lot for that, but the priests still found enough forgiveness in their hearts to allow us to continue attending Mass.

Pam, when she was little, was deathly afraid of Santa Claus. Show her a Santa Clause mask, and she immediately went into hysterics. Now, what two brothers could resist that? Bill and I knew that the Santa Claus costume was kept in a chest in the attic. Every so often, one of us couldn't stand it any longer, and journeyed to the attic and made our sister go nuts. Needless to say, we got spanked by Mother a lot.

At our kindergarten, each class had a musical revue. I can remember playing the triangle for my show. Pam's show was priceless. She and the other little girls came on stage wearing native costumes, each holding a rice tray, and sang this song:

"Planting rice is no fun.
Bend from morn to the set of sun.
Cannot stand and cannot sit.
Cannot rest for a little bit."

(Of course, this had to be sung using a Filipino accent).

My school put on shows also. I had to sing "My Grandfather's Clock" for the assembly, and I would not go on stage unless Betty would go on with me. The school put on a couple of shows for radio, and we sang a lot of patriotic songs, which were well received. This was just before the United States and Japan went to war, but war was already raging in Europe. The radio station was air-conditioned. That was the first time in Cebu that I had ever been cool. I swore that when I grew up, I would have air-conditioning in every room of the house.

Bill and I had Lionel trains that we were only allowed to bring out at Christmastime. They were very expensive, and we were always supervised when we played with the trains. We each were given a large Chris Craft speedboat that was motored by a key like a clock. We didn't see much of those either. We did have "put put" boats that were powered by candles, and we floated those in the bathtub. Japan produced a lot of toys made of thin tin and stamped made in USA, which, as everyone knew, was a town in Japan. Most things made in Japan were junk. The toys didn't last very long, especially the toy swords, which were very easy to bend and were very light. They were not Samurai swords.

Bill and I had Daisy BB guns, the same ones that Red Rider and Little Beaver used in the movies. Bill got his first on his birthday, which completely destroyed me. I moped around during his birthday party until Dad finally noticed and took me aside and asked what was wrong. I told him it was the BB gun. He said that I was going to get one on my birthday, and I tearfully reminded him that was nine long months away. Dad learned that day that with something as momentous as BB guns, both brothers had to get them at the same time to avoid bad feelings and jealousy. I happily got a BB gun the next day.

At our Boromeo house, next to the convent and monastery, we had geckos that loved to climb to the roof of our living room, which was open on three sides, and hunt for insects. Bill and I would shoot them with our BB guns, and they would die stuck to the ceiling. Dad would sometimes borrow our guns and have a go at them too. During the night, we could hear a "plop" as dead geckos hit the floor.

Once, Bill and I went bird hunting with several of our friends. We shot the birds and tried to cook them over an open fire. They never were much good because we never cooked them long enough. Besides, a kingfisher or blue jay doesn't make much of a meal.

We saw a lot of sparrows perched on a telephone line. Bill fired at them and somehow hit the line instead. The birds were immediately electrocuted, and all fell to the ground. One of our friends got so excited that his BB gun went off, and the pellet hit Bill in the forehead. If Bill hadn't been wearing his pith helmet, he could have been seriously hurt.

We didn't have or know about Swiss Army knives. In my day, it was Boy Scout knives. I think they only had three blades, and maybe a bottle opener too. We were very pleased to get them. Dad took us out to the shed for instruction, and I promptly nicked my neck. Bill and I had to say good-bye to our knives for a couple of years.

We also had a little scooter car that could be peddled on the sidewalk. On Opon, we had lots of paved walks, and I usually got to push Bill around. Peddling that little car around was hard work.

We had a tennis court on Opon, but hardly anybody used it. Mostly we would go to the metal posts holding the net and spin the wheels to watch little lizards run out. We did play a lot of badminton, and I got rather good at it. Bill played tennis in high school, and I learned from a friend after I had graduated from high school. My friend never beat me. After the war, Mabel Reed gave Bill a tennis racket. It was the first one I had ever seen that was all metal, including the strings.

We lived for my first six years on Mactan Island in the city of Opon within the Philippine Refining Company's compound. Later we moved to the main island of Cebu.

We traveled to the island of Cebu on various watercraft. Sometimes it was on the company's Chris Craft speedboat, the *Miss Pricilla*. It had two open cockpits forward and aft. There was always a sailor onboard, dressed in whites, to handle the lines, put out the fenders, or do whatever tasks the bosun's mate requested. That sailor would stand between the two open cockpits to handle the lines when we docked. I always thought of him as a romantic figure.

Sometimes we would take the slower and larger launch, the *Visraco*. And sometimes we even had to resort to traveling on a banca, which was a native two-outrigger watercraft. It was extremely exciting when there was little wind, and one outrigger rode high in the air.

Bill and Bob with Jack and Betty Padgett on a banca

When we docked in Cebu harbor, we went by company car to school. Once, when Betty and Jack were with us, we asked Simone to go really fast over a bump in the road, and we would all fly up into the air and fall back in a heap on the floor, laughing all the way.

In Cebu, everybody spoke English around us. Mother did not allow us to speak the native tongue. Of course we learned the swear words and several catch phrases. We were not allowed to eat the native food but did sample the famed fish heads and rice, which were really anchovies and rice. We loved fried bananas at the market, frozen ice cubes, and my all-time favorite, *bud bud* (sic). *Lechon* was barbecued pig.

Bill and I finished off the leftover drinks one night and got deathly ill. We tried cigarettes also and found them not to our liking. Both Mom and Dad had good voices, as do Pam and I. I sang lead soprano in our school choir.

On our last vacation before the war (either 1936 or 1937), we visited our mother's sister, Auntie Mabel, who was living at 377 S. Hudson St. in Pasadena, California. Dad had to go to the Mayo Clinic, and Mother went with him, leaving us kids in the charge of Auntie Mabel. We had a housekeeper named Mrs. Sloan, whose favorite saying was, "You can wait for the potatoes, but the potatoes cannot wait for you." Our amah, Mary, was with us. Auntie Mabel was very nice, but she had no idea what to do with three kids. She was the director of Broadoaks Academy, an acclaimed preschool in Pasadena, which was later moved to Whittier College when she began teaching there. Auntie Mabel had a two-passenger car, and was dating a police officer at that time. Bill and I attended the local grammar school during our stay, and the course of study was a couple of years behind our school in Cebu. I remember the kids tried to pick on me because I was different, and I spent a lot of time in the principal's office for fighting. Bill never seemed to have the same problems that I did. He always got along with everybody despite being a hyperactive child.

When we left Pasadena for our trip home, we rented a seven-passenger Packard, the finest American car of its day, and drove cross-country to catch our ship leaving from California.[1] We had a lot of fun until Pam fell out of the car. The weather had turned cold, and we were all wearing heavy leather and wool jackets, which probably saved Pam's life. We watched her rolling along the highway, but her coat protected her, and she only received some minor cuts and bruises on her bare legs, although her socks were ground into her insteps when she lost her shoes. We had to stop at a doctor's office to bandage her. Mother hit a cow during our journey too. Both the cow and car were none the worse for wear. The best thing about our trip was staying in new lodging called an auto park or motel. It was in a motel that we used an elevator for the first time.

We sailed home on the SS *McKinley*, which was a Dollar Line luxury liner. Traveling first class had its privileges. I could have played on that electric horse in the exercise room all day long. Playing ring toss and shuffleboard daily was a real treat. The ship visited Hong Kong, Peking, and Shanghai, where we picked up the new carpets for our Cebu home. Bill and I were able to rent our own rickshaws to race against each other. We visited Tokyo and stayed for a couple of days. I remember taking a nap in a room dominated by a huge red devil in a home we were visiting. When we got back to the ship, Bill engaged in a duel with our cabin steward and wound up cutting his hand with a tin sword he had picked up in Japan. I clearly remember the ship's captain's son, Huffy, threatening to have me thrown overboard over some altercation between the two of us. I nervously hid under the bed for several hours until he calmed down. I thought he had the authority to do it.

Dad resigned from the Philippine Refining Company, now simply called PRC, over a personal dispute with the head office. We moved to the big island of Cebu, and Dad rented a house from the Noaks on Mango Avenue, which was right down the street from our friends Cap and Charlotte Martin, and the Reeds. Our schoolmate was Mary Rhoda Reed; she always insisted we include Rhoda. The capitol of Cebu, conveniently named Cebu City, was a little farther down the way from our house. Mango Avenue was a broad street with rapid traffic. The house was elevated, with the entire bottom floor open; we lived on the top floor. It was a large house with a balcony that surrounded all sides. One feature Bill and I really liked was the completely tiled back bathroom. We would soap the floors and slide to our hearts content. People thought it was rather strange that we liked to bathe so much. The top of the house was infested with rats and mice, and if we had rats and mice in the Philippines, we got snakes at no extra cost. Sometimes we would see snakes coiled in the rafters, and there was always a lot of slithering going on (especially at night). We always slept under mosquito netting, although one would inevitably get in with us.

There was a huge yard, which was terraced on several levels. There were some large mango trees, which, as any boy will tell you, are the best climbing trees. They have broad, sturdy trunks and branches. Guava trees were also good to climb. One Christmas, we had several friends over and stole some fine cigars that Dad kept in a red Chinese cabinet. We all climbed into our favorite mango tree, lit up, and puffed like crazy. The servants could see the smoke coming out of the tree and couldn't wait to tell on us. Dad did not berate us because he had hoped that the cigars would make us sick. They did not affect Bill and me, although a couple of my buddies turned green and got very sick.

Cebu City entertained an international community, and our little group comprised about 150 of our closest friends. The majority of the expatriates were American, with British, Dutch, German, Spanish, Swiss, Norwegian, Russian, and French rounding out the group. Dad also included the Spanish people who were living there, but the other group members never accepted them. We all did a lot of the same things, went to the same parties, joined the same clubs, and went to our beach club at Liloan, which was about twelve miles from Cebu City. There we could get terribly sunburned, paddle our own banca, and get a real sarsaparilla (not root beer).

Birthday parties were big deals in my day. All the kids came, which meant that we got at least two dozen presents. Weddings were big events too, although I got tired of always being the trainbearer. Those tuxedos were hot and sticky. Everyone loved costume parties. One year Bill and I went as Prince Valiant and Prince Arn. Dad had our swords and shields made in the company shop, and Mother did a great job on our costumes (beat the heck out of my old devil costume).

All my friends lived in nice homes, had plenty of servants, had nice cars to drive, took nice vacations, and seemed to have enough money for everything. We were escorted to the movies by servants, and drank sodas at the Botica Boy drugstore. We even took tap dancing lessons until they ran the instructor out of town for being a *bine baye* (homosexual). Our clothes were all tailor-made. Boys got long pants when they were twelve, and the girls got long "party" dresses. Although some of our parents had more money than others, we kids all shared one thing in common: we never had a dime because we did not need any money, since everything was already taken care of. We passed bicycles from one kid to the other as we outgrew them. They were repainted and given to the kid who just happened to be the next oldest in our group. We played checkers, chess, bridge, Monopoly, Parcheesi, Chinese checkers, and other board games. Card games such as hearts, canasta or crazy eights had not been invented yet.

Bob in his devil's costume with Pam and Bill

Saturday was the best day of the week. We didn't have homework, so the whole day was open. Birthday parties were always held on Saturday. We could play with our friends, go to the club, go hunting with our BB guns, fight with everybody, ride our bicycles, or fly our model airplanes. It was a good life.

Jack Padgett and Bill waiting for their joint birthday party to begin

The joint birthday party in full swing

We liked going to Mother's store, the Brink's Peseta Store, basically a five and dime store, to play with the new toys in the stockroom. Mr. Hessenbergher, the store manager, never liked to have us around much.[2]

Occasionally, we would go to the office with Dad, who was president of the El Dorado Oil Company, or go with him to one of his *bodegas*. We had fun climbing on the copra bags, which were piled almost to the ceiling. *Bodegas* were usually cooled by a little native boy who sat on the floor and pulled a cord attached to pulleys that made a carpet swing back and forth over the area to be cooled. The *bodegas* were near the loading dock scales that Dad owned.

We went to a barbershop on the same street as Dad's office. Right outside there always seemed to be an old Chinese man who had a monkey perched on his shoulder going through his hair looking for lice.

We had roller skates to ride that were not like the roller blades of today. They were metal platforms with wheels attached that would not fit on tennis shoes. We had to use a dress shoe with firm soles and heels. They clamped on the sole and were tightened with a roller skate key. Of course, the skates would always come off when we were going very fast down the sidewalk. Skates were not good on the street.

Once, after a bunch of us kids had come back to the house after watching a western movie, we decided to hang somebody to see what it was like. Billy Hanaford, who was the youngest and smallest guy in our group, said he was willing; so we hoisted him up. His feet kicked up a storm, and we quickly let him down. We never realized that he could have died, and, boy, did I get spanked for that one. It's funny: the guy in the movie didn't seem any worse for wear when we saw him in the next cowboy picture.

I remember Paul Kirkendall fondly. He always wore a white handkerchief in the left pocket of his shirt. In our softball games, he would run the bases with one hand firmly protecting that handkerchief. He always seemed to stay clean while the rest of us got dirty.

The only thing we ever needed money for was to buy model airplanes that we constructed in the garage. An X-Acto knife (which would last forever), paint, and glue were all we ever needed. Bill always built the biggest model. The last model he built was an Aeronca biplane. Mine was a Stuka dive-bomber. The models were designed to fly by rubber band power. We wound them up and let them fly. When we got tired of the models, we would go up on the roof, set the plane on fire, and watch it auger in.

I had a temper, and I could get angry at the drop of a hat. At school, I would often just blow my top and chase all the other kids around the schoolyard. They would run away from me shouting, "Bob is having one of his mad spells." More often than not, it was just a game we all enjoyed. Bill and I were constantly fighting, so Dad put up a boxing ring in the backyard and got us some gloves. We went at each other every day. Woe to the classmate who ever came over to play. He had to put on the gloves, and Bill and I whaled the tar out of him. Any time anyone wanted to fight with Bill, he had to contend with me first. They never got past me. We never fought girls, although I would have made an exception for an older, fat girl named Norma Talmadge who would sit on me until I calmed down.

I seemed to always have scabbed knees. It seemed that every time I wore long pants and rode my bike, the pants would somehow get tangled up in the bike chain. Bill had a large Japanese bike, and I had a smaller American one with fat tires. Bill could ride like the wind. All bikes were one speed in my day.

School was an important part of our young lives. Filipinos, with mostly Spanish colonists' blood, went to school with us. We all attended the Sambag Grammar School for kindergarten. Our teacher was Mrs. Wislizenus (who was the principal). We had such a hard time pronouncing her name that we called her Mrs. Judge instead because her husband had been a judge. He was the director, as well as the president, of the University of the Philippine campus (our local junior college).

When we graduated from kindergarten, we attended the Cebu American School (which is still there today—only now it is called the Cebu International School. One of my old playmates, Josephina "Jo" Aboitiz-Booth, married an army colonel she had met after Cebu was liberated and is currently the principal.) Back then, the school consisted of two rooms: first through fourth grades in one room and fifth through eighth grades in the other. There would be four desks in a row with a hole in each one of them for the inkbottle. The lid lifted up to store books. The school had a large veranda in front and two bathrooms. The teaching staff consisted of Miss Palmer for the older kids and Mrs. Tess Landon for the younger kids. We had great fun spying on Miss Palmer when she went out on dates. We had a full-time janitor who was always handy when we had to shoo away the crazy people who occasionally harassed us. The Japanese sent their children to a school right down the street from ours. Those kids dressed in uniforms: a white shirt and blue pants for the boys and blue skirts for the girls. Everyone had a leather knapsack for their books. The boys at my school all wore white shirts and white short pants and the girls wore anything they wanted. We always wore formal black shoes. Tennis shoes were strictly for play.

Children of the American School at the radio station August, 1940: *left to right, front row*: Jimmy Milling, Janet, Billy Hannaford, Evangeline Hawk, Pam Brink, Lucy Goebel, Margie Cleland, Luisito Aboitiz, (the next might be Lucy Ann Goebel); *second row*: Bobsie Rigby, Ernesto Aboitiz; *back row*: Mary Lou Cleland, Charlie Goebel, Betty Padgett,

Katherine Doner, Jack Padgett, Mary Rhoda Reed, Bob Brink, Bill Brink, Josephine Aboitiz, and someone who seems hiding in the back.

We attended school from eight in the morning until twelve noon, with one fifteen-minute recess. All the older kids participated in softball and volleyball. We knew no other games and did not have the equipment for them anyway. Jack Padgett introduced us to football, and we played by rules that were never clear. We were passed an eraser and ran like crazy for the goal line until everyone tackled us. After a couple of kids lost their teeth, the game was banned. I remember we had slides and swings for the younger children. The Filipino kids liked to come to our school to play, and, when we would see them, a big fight would break out, which we always won. One kid pulled a knife on Bill, but the other boy's grandfather intervened and took the knife away.

After school, we went home, had lunch, went down for our siesta, and then went out to play until teatime. After tea was served, we did our homework. Dad checked our math and Mother checked the rest. By the time Dad finished helping me with my math, we were both worn out and frustrated. Dad liked to translate the word problems into algebra, and that was just too much for me. He would say, "You will learn this by blood, sweat, and tears, just like I did." I don't know about the blood and the sweat, but there were plenty of tears.

In1941, we had a large enrollment of twenty-four students. I was going to be in the fifth grade and finally one of the big kids in school. In order to pass from the fourth grade to the fifth, we had to know our multiplication tables, have memorized one long poem (I chose "The Charge of the Light Brigade," a school favorite), and memorize a history timeline that started at 1200 BC with Cheops and the Great Pyramid and extended all the way to the present time, which meant the end of World War I. Of course, it wasn't called that then; we called it The Great War.[3] I did pretty well in English and liked history, geography, and poetry but could not stand math. (I still shudder at trying to figure out when two trains that left at different times from different points will run into each other—although, I would sure like to see that!) I learned to read by myself the year Betty Padgett went on vacation.

When we finished grammar school, some American students would be sent to the States. If we were British, we might be sent to England to continue our education. If we were Catholic, off we would go to attend one of the Catholic schools. Many families chose to send their children to Brent High School in Baguio, which was a resort near Manila. Bill and I both knew we were slated to attend a military academy located on the East Coast of the United States when it came time to further our education.

This was going to be my year. I was finally joining the big kids in Miss Palmer's room. I was promoted to the fifth grade. Our school had the largest enrollment ever, twenty-four children. I had passed the dreaded timeline to graduate from the fourth grade.

My parents had built a cabin in the mountain town of Montalongon because, at thirty-six hundred feet above sea level, it was a lot cooler there in the summertime. Mother and we kids spent every summer vacation there. It was rather isolated, but we loved it. Dad would usually work in Cebu City during the week and then come up on the weekends.

Montalongon is located in the southern part of Cebu. It was little more than a wide spot in the road with a few *tiendas* and a sponsored market day every Thursday. (Bill's memoir says market day was Wednesday—a good example of how our memories become distorted over the years.) Because the three of us kids were very blonde, we suffered through the natives patting our hair and saying, *"Muy guapa,"* (very pretty!) when we went through town on market days. There always seemed to be a pig squealing that we could hear for kilometers.

The cabin was built out of wood and had no style whatsoever. My Dad drew the blueprints freehand on our dining room table. It had six rooms: A living room/dining room, Mother and Dad's bedroom, a bedroom that could hold four adults, our bedroom that had four bunk beds, a kitchen, and a bathroom. The house was elevated, as were most houses in the Philippines, and we had a pantry under our parents' bedroom. The top of a small hill was shaved off to build the house and fence in the property. The servants lived in a nipa house adjacent to ours. The duck pen was next to their lodgings. There was a coal deposit located in a small cave on the property. There was no electricity. Simone and Sacchi erected a windmill that provided sporadic electricity as long as the wind blew and the windmill didn't blow down. We used Coleman lanterns for light. We had no running water. We had large cisterns at the four corners of the tin roof to collect rainwater. The water tank was rigged with a garden hose that flowed into either the tin bathtub or wash basins. The commode was just that: a toilet seat over a five-gallon can that was dumped each day. Water was heated in the kitchen's woodstove and brought to the bathroom to fill the galvanized iron tub for our weekly Saturday night baths. The servants bathed in the stream right down from our property.

On the front steps of our house in Montalongon: Bob in the back, Pam standing, Bill in front with a friend and her daughter

They were always improving the road in Montalongon and used a lot of dynamite. The crew would blow a whistle, and we would crawl under the dining room table, wait five minutes, and then the blast would come. One day Mother had some friends over to enjoy some "toddies," and one of her friends told her she saw Bill and me climbing the face of the cliff above the road. Mother got out the binoculars and saw us halfway up. We got spanked for that. In fact, we got swatted just about every day just on general principles. Luckily for us, Mother didn't spank very hard.

Dad and Mother had friends visit us at Montalongon all through the summer. Dad had a couple of his bachelor friends visit one day, and when one of them saw that Bill and I had some balsa wood airplanes, which were propelled by rubber bands, he took Bill's and kept winding the propeller, all the while getting the rubber band tighter and tighter. Dad told him that if he let it fly, he would have to go after it. He let it go, and fly it did. It caught some great thermals, and off it went far into the distance. Dad, true to his word, made him go get it. Bill went with him, and they were both gone for hours.

Bill and I were constantly on the move immediately after breakfast when we were on vacation. We had a lot of caves to explore, cliffs to climb, and rivers to ford. Friendly farmers would give us a piece of sugarcane to quench our thirst. We discovered a nice swimming pool with a little waterfall without the requisite leeches. We would make little bancas out of banana leaves and stalks, install sails, and send them downstream.

If any adult came up to stay during the week, we prevailed on them to read to us. Our favorite books were by Frank Baum. (The Oz series—come to think of it—they were the science fiction of children stories.) We could always get Dad to read to us after supper, and he fed us on a steady diet of Edgar Allen Poe. There was no other entertainment on vacation. Dad felt that the radio was for news only, and we were not allowed to touch it.

Our school had a curriculum designed to be home taught in case of unforeseen delays, which came with living in the tropics. We kept up with our schoolwork even during vacation. Mother, a former teacher, would design the curriculum, and Dad would review our math with us on the weekend. Even though I was the dumb one in arithmetic, I knew my father loved me anyway.

Dad had tried growing a garden there every summer. It was an economy measure, but I think it was really a kind of hobby. We grew watermelons among the other fruits and vegetables; and just before they were ready for harvest, all our crops disappeared. The natives who lived close by always seemed to wear a guilty look around harvest time.

The Borromeos, a good Spanish family, had a house near our cabin. A Dutch couple, the Horsestinks, had a cabin near us as well. The Horsestinks were both fat, drank gin constantly, smoked both cigars and pipes, spoke English with a heavy accent, and were very nice and kind. "The shickens are shitting under the zink," was our favorite Horsestinks' phrase.

Our pet ducks would go down to the stream in precise single file every night. We also had a pet cow, at least we thought she was a cow until somebody told us that "she" was actually a "he." "Bessie" quickly became "Besso." That bull was so tame he followed us around just like a dog. We also had Jerry, our German Shepherd, who would stay out at the cabin year around. He was very intelligent and, like most dogs of his breed, was a one-family dog. Jerry was a big black male with very expressive brown eyebrows. His parents' offspring were in demand all over the islands. Jerry's job was first and foremost to be a watchdog, and, therefore, he was not trained to do tricks. His job was to guard the estate at all costs. We all loved him. He was a prince.

We also had fighting cocks or, as some of my friends called them, "fighting chickens." The natives would shave the comb of the rooster so it would not get in the way while fighting, and small knives would be attached to the cock's spurs. Once one of the cocks bit the other cock in the ear, the fight was on. The losing cock went to the winner's owner for supper. We just let our own cocks spar and practice. Pam had a little rooster named "Chickie." We would train him by making him look at himself in a hand mirror. As soon as he saw himself, his little ruff would go up, and he would immediately peck away at the "other" chick.

Maybe that is why I never liked chicken very much. Free-range chicken is very tough and hard to eat. We had to boil them for hours just to make the meat tender. Mary, our cook, would chop the heads off of the chickens and then let them run around just like, well, chickens with their heads cut off. (Lots of fun to watch.) Our turkeys would be fed a couple shots of whiskey, hung upside down on a clothesline, and, after they were thoroughly drunk, they would lose their heads.

Pam's Description of Family Life Prewar

There were five of us: my father, Myron Edgar Brink; my mother, Maude Elizabeth Rice Brink; my two brothers, John William and Robert Arlington; and I, Pamela Jane, the youngest. My parents met and married (1928) in the Philippines. Both had accepted jobs as teachers in the American schools. (Since the Philippines was an American colony at that time, many American businesses were in the islands. The businessmen brought their families with them, so schooling was provided to their children. In those days, it was important for American schoolchildren to be taught by American teachers.) When my parents met, my father was manager of the Lever Brothers affiliate, the Philippine Refining Company, and my mother was the superintendent for English for all the Philippine Islands.

My father came from Parkston, South Dakota, and went to the Philippines directly after finishing college. He was a mathematician and discovered he had a talent for languages.

My mother was from Stephens Point, Wisconsin. She was a normal school graduate and a grade school teacher. She was living in Milwaukee when her sister, Mabel Rice, called and asked her if she would like to go to the Philippines. My aunt had received a job offer to go to the Philippines to teach in the American schools, but she was doing something very interesting in Washington, DC, and did not want to leave her job. She wondered if my mother would be interested instead. Mother decided it would be an adventure and said yes. Neither of my parents ever regretted their decisions.

Bill, Bob, and I were all born in Cebu City on the island of Cebu. Bob wrote a good introduction to our family, who they were and how they came to be in the Philippines.

Engagement of a Popular Couple

A recent engagement has been announced between Miss Maude E. Rice and Mr. Myron E. Brink. For the last three years Miss Rice has been in the Philippines as a superintendent of private schools. She is well known in social and educational circles. Mr. Brink has lived in the Philippines for several years and is the manager of the Philippine Refining Company in Cebu. The wedding will take place in the near future

---

My Parents' wedding party

Back row: *left to right*: Dr. Pond, the family physician who gave the bride away; Morrie Cleland Jr., best man; Myron Brink, groom; Maude Rice, bride; Harriet Richards, matron of honor; and Dr. Dunlop, who officiated at the wedding. Front row: *left to right*: flower girls Carmen

Nutter, Julia McVean, Frances Williamson, Maria Louisa Aboitiz, and Daphne Palmer. Ring bearer Teddy Richards. Branny Richards and Eugene McAdam, train-bearers.

Mother and Dad as newlyweds

As manager of the Philippine Refining Company, my father was allocated living quarters on Mactan Island in the city of Opon, just off

Cebu. To reach Cebu, we had to take the company launch. The house we lived in was a huge two-story affair with the living and dining rooms on the first floor and the bedrooms on the second. The most memorable feature of the house was the openness of the central area, where we children could look through the railings on the second floor balcony and watch the parties below. In addition to the interior balconies, there was one that completely encircled the house on the outside. The outdoor veranda gave access to the mango trees that grew next to the house. The boys would climb up on the railings and see how far out they could reach for a mango before falling off. That all ended when we were caught.

Our house on Opon

All the company homes on the island were completely private, screened from each other by landscaping. We children would walk from home to home without having to go out on the road. From our house, down the sloping lawn to the channel between Opon and Cebu, was the swimming pool where my father taught us to swim. (As a child, I never differentiated between the island of Mactan and the city of Opon. As far as I was concerned it was all Opon.) Bob also mentions the swimming pool my father had built. Several pictures were taken in and around the pool. In one picture, the two amahs were sitting poolside with their small charges.

At poolside: *left to right*: Raphael Tumalock,
Bill, Bob, Pam, and Mary Tumalock

I was about three years old when we moved from this wonderful compound to the Noaks house (the former owners) in Cebu City. Again, we lived in a large two-storied house surrounded by extensive treed grounds. I had my fourth birthday party at the Noaks house, where my invitation list consisted entirely of my father's business colleagues. At the Noaks house, we lived across the street from one of my classmates, Normie Naylor, and his brother, Billy. We were wormed when we lived at the Noaks house. We had to drink some nasty-tasting stuff. As I was coming home from Normie's one day, I felt something wiggling in my underpants. I ran to my room and took off my pants to find a very large worm. Evidently the medicine worked very well.

Although the United States was undergoing a severe depression in the 1930s, it had little impact on the lives of expatriates in the Philippines. The salaries for the managers and CEOs of companies allowed for a lifestyle that would have been impossible in their home countries. There were servants for every household task from cook and chauffeur to gardeners, *lavanderas,* maids, and amahs for the children. We lived a life of privilege.

After work, the men would play golf or tennis, swim, or go to a party at the country club. The women were the school teachers, Sunday school teachers, gave or attended bridge or tea parties, and went out in the evenings with their husbands. (The other mothers would not allow my mother to teach Sunday school because she was a Catholic.) I didn't see much of my father in those days except at meals, dinners at our house, or during holidays. My parents did a lot of entertaining. Mother told me that both General MacArthur and General Eisenhower were dinner guests when we lived on Opon, but they were aides to generals at the time and not particularly noticed.

On Sundays, we went to the beach at Liloan. We stayed all day and always came home with severe sunburns. One time, Bobsie Rigby was badly bitten by a jellyfish. He screamed with the pain and had to be taken back to town to see the doctor.

When we left the Noaks house, we moved into my favorite house, the Boromeo house. What a beautiful house. The grounds were not as extensive as those at the Noaks house, but it was a beautifully planned house with a circular driveway. It was two-storied, with the ground floor containing, on the right of the front entrance, an open porch that reached to the end of the house, which served as the living room. On the left was the formal dining room and behind it the kitchen. Mother and Dad entertained on that open porch, and we had a small informal dining table at the back where we ate Sunday breakfast. The front door opened into a foyer with a staircase that began on the right, then became a landing halfway up. The stairs then proceeded up on the left to the second floor. Upstairs were four bedrooms, two on the left separated by a bathroom, and two on the right, again separated by a bathroom. My brothers and I had our bedrooms on the left. Mother and Dad each had their own bedroom on the right.

Behind the house were some guava and mango trees that were perfect for climbing. I broke my arm falling out of the biggest guava tree when I was seven. My father bought a horse for my brother Bob to learn to ride. For a little girl who loved to climb trees, I found the height of a horse frightening. He was a mean-minded horse with a tendency to bite unexpectedly

It was at the Boromeo house that Dad brought home a six-month-old German Shepherd puppy, which Mother named Jerry. Dad had given Mother a German Shepherd puppy as a wedding present, but Guapa died while we were still living on Opon. Dad had found this puppy at the home of a Dutch couple who were German Shepherd breeders. They were willing to give Jerry up when they found he had severe hip dysplasia. Mother came home from the store one afternoon as we all gathered around to see her response to Dad's gift. At first, she didn't see him hiding under a chair. Jerry was black except for his tan eyebrows, which were the only things that could be seen. It was, as they say, love at first sight for both of them. My mother had a remarkable affinity for animals. She and Jerry bonded immediately.

We also had cats, which were better at protecting our property than Jerry was. We began with two, and ended with twenty-seven. No animal ever dared enter our grounds. The entire band of cats would attack simultaneously, sending the unsuspecting dog whining out the gate with cats on his back, at his heels, and leaping at his face. The cats always left the intruder at the gate.

The Borromeo house was on a corner. On one side, across the street from us, was the Catholic seminary where Mother would go to Mass every Sunday. I believe it was a Redemptorist seminary. Across the street at the front of the house was the convent and girls' boarding school run by Belgian nuns. I believe they were the School Sisters of Notre Dame. Mother insisted that I take piano lessons from the nuns. I was not particularly interested, but Bill was. He couldn't take lessons, as it was a school for girls only. So I used to share my lessons with him when I got back from my lessons.

We had private Spanish lessons from a senorita. We were taught Castilian, which we had to drop when we took Spanish in California. I was able to pick up a decent Spanish accent but never picked up much vocabulary. (My mother mentions the senorita in her letter dated 1939.)

Our doctor was Doctor Ramos. His office was very large with shelves of embalmed animals. He also had one or two human babies in large glass jars. Later my brother Bill told me that one of the babies was our brother who was dead at birth. I can only imagine how my mother felt going to Dr. Ramos's office and seeing her baby in a jar.

From the Borromeo house we moved once again, this time to the Millings' house, which was on the main highway and next door to the junior college. Although I don't remember when we moved or why, a letter from my mother to her mother and sister, dated September 6, 1941, describes the house as if it were new for her. The Millings had left for the United States. I was not happy with the move. The Millings' house was a two-story house set way back from the street with a long driveway leading up to the garage. From the drive, one climbed to the second floor via an outdoor staircase to the entry, which was a long screened porch across the front of the house. The porch opened directly into the central formal dining room, which separated the bedrooms—two on each side. One of the bedrooms on the left had been converted into a small open *sala.* I slept in the rear bedroom on the right, and my parents had the front right bedroom. Our bedrooms were separated by a bathroom with a stall shower. My brothers were on the other side of the dining room. The kitchen was behind the dining room, at the back of the house. On the ground floor of the house were the garage, laundry, and servants' bedrooms. The huge front lawn had many trees, and housed the greenhouse my mother had built for her orchid collection. Everywhere she went on the islands, she would bring back at least one wild orchid.

One day, Mother was having friends over for bridge. One woman came down the drive and, spotting my best friend Evan (Evangeline Hawk) and me, asked us who we were, as she hadn't met us before. She wondered if we had been invited to tea. We were dressed up in my mother's clothes, hats, and shoes. We were so excited that she had not recognized us! What a special thrill for two little girls.

Margie Cleland asked me if I wanted to ride our bikes in the morning before school. Since Lahug Avenue was a busy street most of the time, we had to ride before morning traffic began. Evidently, Margie and her family also lived off Lahug. Margie gave up on me when I overslept once too often.

One day when Mary Cleland came to tea with her baby, Maureen, a blanket was put down on the floor for Maureen to crawl on. Our dog, Jerry, was fascinated by Maureen but was told he could not get on the blanket with her. So, lying on his stomach, he inched his way toward Maureen until the tips of his toes were touching the blanket. Then Maureen solved the problem. She crawled over to Jerry and tried to crawl up on his back. He slowly got up with her clutching his fur. She took her first steps clinging to Jerry. No one ever worried about him again.

I was, and remain, profoundly left-handed. When I was in kindergarten at the Sambag Grammar School, Mrs. Judge (who was the principal) would come into classrooms unexpectedly to see what was going on. If she caught me writing with my left hand, she would rap smartly on the back of my hand with the ruler she carried all the time. Even in the third grade, when I broke my left arm and was in a cast for what seemed like forever, I simply could not write with my right hand. It was a struggle to get illegible squiggles. Finally, everyone stopped trying to make me right-handed.

The American School was down the highway from the Millings' house. It was a two-room school with one room for the first four grades, while the other held grades five through eight. My brother Bill was in the eighth grade. There were no high school facilities for expatriates, so children were usually sent to a boarding school (either to Manila, the United States, or England).

I had asthma attacks periodically for no discoverable reason. Mother assumed it was a food allergy, so certain foods were constantly being eliminated from my diet. Nothing helped. It wasn't until decades later that research showed there was a phenomena called "exercise induced asthma." These were excruciating times when I could not get my breath. In those days, the treatment for asthma was to create a smoke out of some kind of medicinal powder, cover the head as one bent over the smoking pan, and inhale the smoke. It made everything much worse, and I had even more trouble getting my breath. I never understood the logic for this medication. I heard that in America they put the powder in something like a cigarette. I wondered if that would have been better.

My very best friend in the third grade was Evangeline Hawk. Her father was the physician for the Shell Oil Company for Cebu. They lived on Shell Island. What wonderful weekends when I was allowed to go and visit Evan. During one of those weekends, I had an asthma attack.

Evangeline's father said he would give me a shot, and, of course, I balked. Every shot I ever had was painful. In those days, needles were reused after being sharpened and autoclaved. But eventually the needles developed little hooks on them, making a shot painful, especially when being withdrawn. So, fearing that pain, I objected as best I could, "No, no, no." He overrode my objections and gave me a shot of epinephrine, which immediately stopped the attack. The shot didn't even hurt! I was so impressed!

Another time Dr. Hawk taught us to dive off the pier. We had been jumping in, but that, he said, would make us break a leg. "Much better to dive head first and break our heads," he said.

Evan and I did lots of wonderful experimenting together. We were allowed to wander freely over the island unaccompanied by an amah. One time we tried to build a house out of palm fronds, but our enthusiasm was not matched by any skill. We would take her old cat to the sea wall and drop it, turning it on its back or letting it fall feet down. Evan was right; the cat always landed on its feet. Miraculous! We tried to fly by tying towels around our necks and jumping off the end of the bed. We played "Indians" by taking off all our clothes, putting a belt around our waists, and tying tea towels in both front and back. We were caught and were forbidden to leave the house. Worse, we were told we had to wear underpants. We protested vehemently. "The Indians don't wear underpants!" We lost the argument.

Our family had a home in Montalongon in the mountains above Cebu where we went during holidays. It was a long, narrow, battleship gray house on stilts with a tin or iron roof. It sat on a hill with a view down toward the river, where our ducks marched single file daily. On the other side of the river was the Filipino market. The front entrance, facing away from the river, was accessed by a short staircase. At the back of the house was a porch where we sat to watch the sunsets and sing. The front door opened to a large open room containing my parents' double bed, chairs in a seating arrangement, a sofa, my mother's sewing machine, and a large round poker table. The kitchen and children's bedroom with two sets of bunk beds opened off this center room. The bathroom was off the children's room. There was no electricity or running water. The toilet seat was over a bucket that had to be emptied. Hurricane lamps were used in the evenings.

My father and brothers often went exploring, and one day my father found the perfect swimming hole. It was a pond formed at the base of a waterfall with a lovely sandy beach surrounded by tropical trees and bushes. Not only was it secluded, there were no leeches! The river below our house was infested with leeches, so it was no fun going swimming there. My father waded into the pool first to "check to see that there were no crocodiles." There weren't, of course, but I always worried about it. My brothers tell me they went to the pool frequently. I only remember going once. One day we were on a hike, probably to the pool, when I had a severe asthma attack and had to go home. That was the end of that trip, and I was never allowed to go again.

We were in school the day the Japanese bombed Pearl Harbor on Monday, December the eighth. (The International Date Line divides Hawaii from the Philippines, which is why it was Monday, December 8, in the Philippines while it was Sunday, December 7, in Hawaii.) Our parents came to get us and take us home. I was in the third grade.

Chapter 2

WAR COMES TO CEBU

Bill's Memories

For us, the children, life went on as usual. I was twelve and in the final months of eighth grade that Monday, December 8, 1941. It was a school day. My fellow students and I went to class as usual. We had just begun when cars began to arrive at school. My brother Bob, my sister Pam, and I were told we were going to our summer home in the mountains at Montalongon. Now. We went. The war had started.

Clark Field (the army base north of Manila) had been attacked. The radio told of Pearl Harbor. Later in the day, a Jap sub surfaced in the channel and lobbed some shells into Cebu City.

Life continued calmly for a while. Dad would commute on weekends. Captain Cushing of the army would come up on his Harley to check on us. I remember the ivory grips on his .45. Father Sheridan, now an army chaplain, came for a visit. Ed Kincaid, an escapee from Bataan, came through before he attempted his try for Australia. Another family, the Mullaneys—Ed, Dorothy, Carol, and Eddy, were staying with us.

Market day was Wednesday in Montalongon. You could hear the pigs squealing for miles as they were carried down the higher mountains into town.

We were brought word one day in March: "The Japs are landing in Dalagete!" We walked to the ridges, where we could see over the edge and down into the tree-covered lowlands and white beaches below. They were!

Several ships were standing off the shore. Barges plied their trade between the beaches and the ships. Aircraft were visible flying over the beach and over the water between the land and the ships. It was interesting and frightening. We walked back to our mountain house.

For a while, we moved farther away from town. Each Wednesday we hid in a cave. Nothing would happen, so we returned to the hill overlooking Montalongon.

Cebu fell in April.

Bob's Memories

By the fall of 1941, we all knew that war was coming. The Germans had conquered all of Europe save for England and Russia; and we felt it was just a matter of time for them. We had many bazaars for the British War Relief. Two of our friends were already fighting the Germans. The Japanese had been fighting with China for the last few years, and we had Russian refugees in Cebu who had escaped the horror of Japanese occupation. We listened intensely to the BBC and Don Bell, "The Voice of the Philippines." (See the reference to Don Bell in the memoir of Claire Wislizenus.) Douglas McArthur, old "Dugout Doug" as we referred to him, was constantly quoted saying that "the Philippines are prepared." Many men had already sent their wives and children home, while many thousands of us expatriates stayed. It seemed inconceivable that the Japanese would be so arrogant to enter into a war with the United States. If they did, we all felt the war would be over in a couple of months. (See the letter from Maude Brink to her sister and mother, September 1941, stating that the family would not be leaving the PI.)

December 8, 1941, began just like any other Monday during my young life; I went to school. Due to the International Date Line, we were one day ahead of the Western Hemisphere. It was just a normal school day until I looked out the window and saw our car just as my mother came rushing into the classroom. She shouted, "The Japanese are bombing Pearl Harbor and are attacking Manila right now! Grab your things and get your books; we are going to Montalongon."

After the initial Japanese attack on Manila, they bombed Cebu harbor as well. My schoolmates were picked up by their families, and everyone scattered. Many went to Busai, some to Camp John Hay, some to White Horse, and, unfortunately, most had no other place else to go and stayed in the city. When we went to Montalongon, we took the Mullaneys, who had recently arrived in the Philippines and did not know many people. Mother, of course, took them under her wing. Ed Mullaney was a big, blustery man who, despite being a former marine, was a dedicated coward. His wife, Carole, was a small, petite woman. Eddie was their only son, as "fearless" as his father, and liked to pick fights with me. Their only daughter, Dorothy, was a small, slow-speaking, brown-haired girl who was a year older than Pam. Needless to say, the cabin was rather crowded.

Since we were fairly isolated, "Big Ed" decided that he would cut our hair. As this was his first attempt at barbering, we all ended up with all of our hair clipped off. One of the most uncomfortable things I can remember was having my hair stick to the pillowcase until it finally grew out.

Eddy was not only four years older than me but was bigger than me as well. He was quick to anger, and that anger was usually directed my way. Although, I do have to admit that I could not stop teasing him, which usually ended in fisticuffs. I was big for my age: five feet tall and a solid one hundred pounds. Eddy was bigger and heavier, but he did not know how to box. His usual strategy was to rush me when I was not looking and rain blows on the crossed arms over my head. In the ring, he was a sucker for anything I threw at him. I could have punched him silly with just one hand. He liked to attack when he knew some adult was nearby so that they could break it up before I started to punch him back. Bill always let me fight my own battles.

We all lived on tender hooks until the day the Japanese finally got to the cabin.

Pam's Memories

When we evacuated Cebu the day Hawaii was bombed, we went to our summer home in Montalongon. We took another family (the

Mullaneys—Big Ed and his wife Carol, his son Eddie, and daughter Dorothy) with us, as they had no place else to go. Eddie was my brothers' age and Dorothy was my age.

While we were waiting for the war to end, Mother tried to make our lives as normal as possible. She insisted on our keeping up with our school work. I found math difficult. Mother made up a deck of flash cards to practice math problems. She would write a math problem on one side of a three by five card with the answer on the reverse. Dorothy would hold up a card with the problem facing me, and I was supposed to give the correct answer. Since she had the correct answer facing her, she knew if I had it right or not. The object was to get the answer correct, quickly. Not being a quick thinker, this exercise was excruciating for me. Dorothy was much better than I was at flash cards.

For the most part, I wasn't interested in clothes and hated getting them as Christmas presents. One thing Mother made for me, with an exact duplicate for Dorothy, was a white, floor-length dressing gown. The gown was tight at the neck, wrists, and waist, with three rows of rickrack at the neck, wrists, and waist. One had red rickrack, and the other had blue rickrack. The material felt like silk. I felt very special and beautiful when I wore that gown.

Dad only turned on the radio for news, so our chief entertainment was reading. Auntie Mabel, my mother's sister, kept us well supplied with books, so we had plenty to read. In the evenings, we would take our chairs out to the back porch, watch the sunset and sing. We had a windup Victrola for playing records. One of our favorite records was "In a Persian Market." It frequently served as a backdrop to the little plays we dreamed up for Mother and Dad. The play I remember best was a sword fight between the boys, complete with towels tied around their necks as cloaks, while I flitted about like a fairy.

Chapter 3

THE DAY THE SOLDIERS CAME

Bill's Memory

One Sunday afternoon later in April, we were taking our usual siesta. Rifle shots sounded, and several times our galvanized iron roof rang with hits. We woke and looked down our little hill. A troop of about forty-five bayoneted Japs were marching toward us.

My father had us sit in a semicircle of chairs facing the front door. Jerry, our Alsatian, was chained to an oak table on a down-stay.

The sound of hobnailed boots up our wooden front steps. The front door was slammed open. Every one of us had a bayonet pointed at our stomachs. Jab, jab, jab. Hoo! Hoo! Hoo! And we were herded out on the front grass.

It was not a pleasant experience later for several members of our group, including the Filipina girls.

Our Lincoln Zephyr was taken. Only six sparkplugs could be found, but it ran. My father was taken as a hostage, and they left. He was never able to talk about that experience, but it gave him nightmares until internment caused his death in 1945. A local native had given the Japs our location.

Bob's Memory

Cebu was finally invaded on April 10, 1942, and our Japanese "guests" finally came calling on us on April 20. Some say that the Japanese had come to Montalongon looking for the governor of Cebu and, finding that he was not at his home, attacked our house instead. The Japs came storming in the front door yelling incomprehensibly in Japanese. They all carried long rifles with the longest bayonets I had ever seen attached to the barrels. It was surreal having a bunch of crazy Orientals screaming at us while jabbing at us with their weapons. None of us spoke Japanese, but we finally understood that the women and children were to go outside and sit under the coconut trees in the front yard while the parents stayed in the house as the Japs ransacked it. Of course, they had full rein to search our cabin to their hearts' content. They were looking for money, jewelry, food, and firearms. They quickly found all of our money in our various hiding places. We had a large supply of canned food in the pantry underneath our parents' bedroom, which became the property of the Japanese. A friend of my parents had been in charge of loading canned goods at the docks, and we always got all the dented cans. The soldiers had already looted canned goods from the local tiendas, and they made sure to bayonet the empty cans so no one could use them.

In a strange testament to the Japanese sensibilities, one little soldier found Mother's sewing box and, with meticulous care, selected a needle and then measured off two lengths of thread. He put them carefully in his shirt pocket, closed the sewing box, and placed it gently back where he had found it.

Bill and I had toy cap pistols that resembled a cowboy's six-shooter. We had replaced the toy gun holsters with real pistol holsters. The Japanese found the holsters and shoved a bayoneted rifle into Ed Mullaney's side yelling, "Pistol!" Although he was unhurt (the bayonet didn't break the skin) he about died of fright. Luckily, the soldiers were finally convinced that we had no weapons (although I don't know what ever happened to the shotgun).

All this time, the women and children were working their way to the edge of the hill in the front of the house to try to get as far away as possible. The Japs finally demanded that one of the men go into Cebu City as a hostage. Dad volunteered even though he was not well at the time. Ed Mullaney silently sat as they led Dad out of the house.

After the Japs left with Dad, we let Jerry out. He went howling and barking out of the house at full speed but stopped at the open gate as we yelled at him to stop. We had to leave Jerry behind with the servants when we were finally forced into the concentration camp. Mary was able to bring him by to visit when we were at the university camp. We found out after the war that he had died of a broken heart.

The native Filipinos were not captured or imprisoned by the Japanese. As a conquered people, their primary job now was obeying the edicts of the Japanese. Luckily for us, their limited freedom helped provide us with concealment, food, and information.

Pam's Memory

The Japanese soldiers came to our mountain home at Montalongon twice. The first time, they took my father with them. The second time, they came for the rest of us. Our lives changed irrevocably.

The day the soldiers came was much like any other. We were having afternoon tea (my brothers said we were having our siesta) when we noticed a caravan of trucks moving slowly along the road up toward our house. The trucks were filled with Japanese soldiers. Bayonets were fixed to their guns. They piled out of the trucks and trudged up the hill toward our house.

As soon as we saw the soldiers, my mother told our dog, Jerry, to get under the big poker table, which was covered with a tablecloth that reached to the floor. She told him to stay. My father went outside to greet the soldiers and find out what they wanted. They wanted all of us to come outside and stand in front of the house with our hands up. Then they took Dad into the house with them, and we could hear things being smashed. Some of the soldiers found our canned goods and opened them with their bayonets. They would take a sip, and then throw the can out the window, leaving the lawn strewn with opened cans. We could hear them shouting "*peestol, peestol*" looking for guns. All we had was Dad's old shotgun with rags hanging from the ends of the barrels. Mother used it when robbers threatened us.

We all stayed outside while the soldiers were indoors. I was with Mary, my amah, who had been slapped unnecessarily by one of the soldiers. My mother sat apart praying the rosary and crying.

Finally, Dad came out of the house with the soldiers. He went over to mother and whispered to her before leaving with the soldiers. He didn't come back.

When we eventually returned indoors, we found they had trashed the house. Clothes had been pulled from closets, schoolbooks were strewn all over the floor, and tables and chairs were upended. Mother released Jerry from his stay command under the poker table, and he dashed to the front gate barking madly. It seemed miraculous to me that Jerry never barked while the soldiers were in the house, so the soldiers had never discovered him.

We had no word about Dad. We had no idea whether he was alive or dead.

Chapter 4

THE TRIP FROM MONTALONGON TO CEBU

Bill's Memoir

About three weeks lapsed for us in worry and anxiety. We had nothing to go by, no way of knowing what was in store for us next.

Then it came. A note hand carried.

"You will come or else." The Japanese Army.

Phil Bunker, an English businessman staying in the mountains with his elderly mother, decided he had better go in, too. Good thing it was for us. He had a Chevrolet sedan, and the Japs had our car. An elderly Dutch couple were neutrals and decided to stay.

The Bunkers' Chevy had gas and plugs, and the battery worked. Two Bunkers, four Mullaneys and four Brinks set out on the ninety-kilometer trip to Cebu City.

The fourteen kilometers down to Dalagete was the only peaceful part of the trip. The streets of Dalagete were still stained with blood where the Philippine Army had fought. We crossed streams where bridges had been destroyed. At every barbed-wire checkpoint, we were met by Japs who couldn't speak English. We showed them the note (see above) they couldn't read.

"In Chick! In Chick!" they would say. They meant were any of us Chinese, as they eyed Ed Mullaney. (I believe today that a positive response would have been disastrous.) That was one nightmare of a trip, and part of it was after dark.

On the outskirts of Cebu City, an officer who could speak English transferred us to the gate of Cebu jail.

Bob's Memoir

After Dad was taken hostage, we were constantly listening for the cry of "Nipponese." When we heard that, we would run through the sugarcane and abaca fields to our cave. Mary, our cook, Ebing's (one of our first amahs) and Rafael's sister, would drop a basket of food and water down from the chimney of our cave when it was safe to do so. We would spend hours waiting in complete silence until we would hear the "all clear" and it was safe to come out. Jerry would, of course, always be with us, and waited just as silently.

With the help of our servants and the natives, we evaded the Japanese patrols for about two weeks. However, on May 3, 1942, we got the word through the "bamboo telegraph" that if we did not come into Cebu City immediately, Dad would be shot.

We had a Lincoln town car that was adequate to transport all of us to the mountains. Before the Japanese could confiscate it, we had hidden the sparkplugs and the tires.[4] We had sold all of our other cars to the army when the war broke out. We were finally paid for them in pesos after the war (even with the bills of sale, we had a devil of a time collecting).

We, reluctantly, began our drive toward captivity (somehow the tires and sparkplugs of our car miraculously appeared; of course, they were just where we had hidden them). We each had packed a small suitcase. Roadblocks of Japanese soldiers were frequent. There was a barricade at the entry and exit of every city and some in between. Each time we were stopped, we were thoroughly searched, and the car was unloaded and our suitcases rifled. Everywhere we looked, it seemed, there were soldiers with bayonets screaming at us in Japanese. Even though Cebu City was only eighty kilometers away, it took us all day and part of the night. We were stopped at Dalagette, Argao, Simonga, Carcar, Fernando, Naga, Minglaniila, Talisay, and finally Cebu City. We arrived at our destination, the Cebu Provincial Jail, a little after 9:00 p.m. The

American Army had burned the city before the Japanese could occupy it, and, although we were not able to see much because the streetlights were all broken, we could tell that the city had been reduced to rubble.

Pam's Memoir

After the soldiers took my father away, we lived in fear of the day when they would come to get us, too. We would get a report from our Filipino friends that the Japanese were coming and scouring the countryside looking for Americans, and we would all go somewhere and hide. Sometimes we would spend the day with friends far from our own house. At one of those times, we discovered what we called "The Cockroach House" because that is what it was; an abandoned house filled with cockroaches. We had a wonderful time stamping all over the cockroaches until we got tired.

Other times when we went away to hide, we went to a cave. I have a picture in my head of a huge open cave with an uneven floor of rocks with an entrance covered with vines so we could not see out and no one could see in. Bill told me the cave was an opening under the roots of a huge tree. Mother sat on a rock, holding onto Jerry and trying to keep him quiet rather than bark at people passing by. I know we were there to hide from the soldiers, but I have no sense of how long we were there. For that, I had to rely on my brothers.

We spent the day in fear listening for every noise, knowing it was the Japanese searching for us. The Mullaneys were with us, huddled in their own space. It was around noon when Mary came with food.

Evidently someone came to tell us the Japanese were gone, and it was safe to come out and go home. It may have been Raphael, Mary's brother, who looked after my brothers and served as general handyman, who came to get us.

So after my father was taken from us by the Japanese and before they came and got us, we spent our time in fear. I am sure we went off hiding at other times as well, but the experiences of the cockroach house and the cave stand out.

The day arrived when the soldiers came to get the rest of us. I was taking a nap when my mother awakened me. Mary helped me dress, and I went into the front room, where Mother was talking to a soldier. She said something very quickly to Mary, who took me back to the bedroom and started putting several dresses on me. It was difficult to walk with all the clothes she put on me. (This is obviously a collapsed memory of the day the soldiers came and the day we left for Cebu.)

I selected two dolls to take with me: my Betsey Wetsy and a handmade Raggedy Ann rag doll that my mother had bought for me at a British War Relief sale in 1939. I kept them with me for the entire time we were in the internment camp, only leaving them behind at our rescue. Mother was still convinced that the war would soon be over, so we only packed enough to last us for a maximum of three months. Three years later, most of these clothes were in shreds or outgrown. Mother's Keds (the most popular tennis shoe at the time) had to have the soles sewn to the tops many times. By the time we were rescued, my brothers and I were wearing shirts and underpants mother had knitted out of string. By then, we were either going totally barefoot or wearing *bakyas* (a wooden clog with a single strap over the toes).

Mother left Mary in charge of the house. Together they hid Mother's diamond engagement ring in the rafters. We learned later that Mary sold it for food. We never begrudged her the ring.

Then we started to leave, and I realized Mary was not coming with us. I couldn't understand why. She had always been with us; even when Mother fired her, she would always come back.

We walked down the hill to the car, and Mother sat in the front with the chauffeur. The rest of us were in the back. Our last view of our home was Mary standing at the gate with Jerry at her side. My mother told me that Jerry never left his post at the gate. He simply sat and waited, refusing both food and water. That was where he died.[5]

It took us a long time to drive to Cebu. We made many stops, and, as usual, whenever we stopped, people would reach into the car to touch my blonde hair. It was dark when we reached Cebu. We drove past faceless buildings, rubble with stairs going nowhere. No one was on the streets.

There was no light because of blackout. We had to navigate past many barricades. A soldier would step out of a small hut and shout at us and wave his gun around. It was a terrifying experience.

When we finally stopped, we were at the city jail. We were shoved out of the car and directed toward a door. We saw my father waiting for us. In the half-light, the shadows from the bars made him look as if he had been beaten. But he smiled a great smile and hugged us all.

We began our lives as prisoners of war of the Japanese, as a family, in the Cebu City Jail. It was to be our first prison camp.

Chapter 5

OUR LIVES AS PRISONERS OF WAR BEGINS

Bill's Story

On the outskirts of Cebu City, an officer who could speak English transferred us to the gate of Cebu jail.[6]

As we entered, we saw American Army officers. Some we knew. We were not allowed to speak to them. Later we learned our doctors were not allowed to treat the injured or wounded.

The prison was filthy. One of my friends came down with the mumps. The weather was warm. Women were separated from men. Some of the girls wore little to sleep in. The guards walked up and down the rooms, so women had to take turns staying awake to watch for trouble.

We were moved out of the Cebu jail in about three weeks. It could be longer or less. My memory does not help. We were taken to the junior college campus. It was a mess. There was no running water indoors, so every wastebasket and bin had been used for toilets. We, of course, had the chore of making it livable. The junior college was across a field from our home in the city.

When mother asked the camp commandant if she could have my sister's clothes, he said, "No, it is impossible." She lost her temper and shook his sword under his nose. He called my father in and told him, "Keep that woman away from me. She's crazy!" (That major had a store across from my mother's store in peacetime. We really expected more of him.)

We watched as our Chinese rugs were taken. We watched as our inlaid nara and camagon antique furniture was taken. We watched as all our books were burned on the front lawn.

The British had been moved to a different camp. Norwegian sailors who were taken from their ship stayed with us. We set up a camp government. Mrs. Doner was in charge of one meal. My mother another. I don't remember who was responsible for the third.

Our men dug and built latrines. They screened and set up showers. Men's were screened between the facilities and the buildings. They were wide open to the outside.

The whole camp community developed a shifty attitude during these months. Roll call was taken twice a day. We would line up in double rows.

"Saskit! Bango!"

Neither Americans nor Norwegians could seem to learn Japanese even when ordered to do so.

"Cor nabba! (count number?)

We did. The rear line would shift slightly. There would be fewer or more prisoners at each count. We would be counted again. This would happen in morning and evening.

We children had good schooling during the years we were well enough to profit from it.

We cleaned the JC too well. We were moved to the Philippine Country Club. It was at the end of the airfield's runway. During a severe storm, one bachelor escaped. The camp guards were notified later in the evening that he had been very sick and delirious and wandered off during the storm. The golf course was thoroughly searched. He got away and joined the guerillas.

Another time during a class day, a Jap bomber took off in a locust swarm. It crashed and burned at our end of the runway. We watched it go in while we cheered. Some general class officers were on board. We also saw fighters come in with holes in their bodies and tails.

Bob's Story

At the outbreak of the war, all Japanese nationals were deemed to be part of the Japanese war machine; and any Jap jailed by the US Army for probable spying was immediately set free. It was their jail that became our first internment camp. The jail looked like a jail. It was completely walled in with guard towers at the four corners of the yard and over the front entrance. We were herded out of the car and marched into the jail accompanied by the nonstop screaming in Japanese. I guess the Japs felt that if they screamed loud enough and jabbed at us with their rifles that they could get their meaning across. That was their modus operandi for the next three years.

A very frightened, pajama-clad, Gene McAdams was ushered to the foyer of the jail. (In my memory, it was our father who met us. I think Bob's account is probably the more accurate.) He thought he was roused out of bed to be shot. Gene had sent his wife, Pansy, home before the war started. Cy Padgett had sent Blanche, Betty, and Jack home to the States. A lot of the younger men, like Morrie Cleland, who had been commissioned in the US Army, had either been captured, had joined the Filipino guerrillas, or had been killed. Cap and Charlotte Martin, our friends who lived down the road from us when we lived in the Noaks house, disappeared into the hills. Gene stoically led us inside into the yard of the jail. Women and children were sent to one jail wing, and men and boys were sent to the other. Bill and I were never considered children because we were as large as most adult Japanese soldiers were. It was in the men's wing where Dad greeted us. We were to share the same cell. At least we all got a cot to ourselves. If we stood on a cot, on our tiptoes, we could see out into Cebu harbor and see all of the damaged and sunken ships.

There was absolutely nothing to do in jail. The jail yard was entirely barren with the exception of a couple of beetle nut palm trees. We used the fallen beetle nuts for toys. There were both red and black ants in the yard, and we would sometimes collect ants from one colony and pour them into the hole of the other just to watch them fight. Most of our fellow internees just milled around.

Every day, more people were being brought into internment at the jail. They would adjust to their confinement in their own peculiar ways. Sir Wally and Louisa Walford, our local British nobility, would still take tea every afternoon at precisely at 4:00 p.m. They didn't have any tea or biscuits, but they made do with just hot water.

Doc Hawk, our family doctor, had enlisted in the US Army when the war broke out and was also a guest at the jail. He set up a clinic and would "pipeline" us with information until we eventually transferred out.

On May 16, 1942, we were transferred out of the jail and transported by truck to the junior college campus. As we had to go through the middle of downtown Cebu City, we went right past Mother's store. The only thing left was the melted safe and some concrete stairs sticking out of the rubble. The University of the Philippines was on Lahug Avenue, which was the same street as our school, many of my playmates' homes, and our last house that was just across the street from the Philippine Military Academy. Evidently, a battle had been fought around the campus. There were slit trenches that we had to fill in, and the ground was extremely contaminated. If we got a scratch, it would develop into a tropical ulcer and would take weeks to heal.

As any normal child, I always had scraped knees. One time, I stepped barefoot onto a bamboo thorn that went right up into my heel. Rebecca "Billie" Self, our camp nurse, put some purple stuff on my sores, but they never healed up until after we left the junior college. Marge Cleland and I found a couple of ceremonial sabers with scabbards, and we buried them under the main building. I went back to retrieve them after the war when I returned to Cebu, but the area had been dug up, and offices had been constructed on our hiding place.

My family was assigned one large room right off the main entrance. Dad's little commissary, where we could buy either native or regular cigarettes and snacks, was on the opposite side of the entrance to a former school office. All families were allowed to stay together. There were no inside toilets, so we had to build "two-holer" outhouses. We had to use old newspapers, from the college archives, for toilet tissue. Adults shared cooking and housekeeping duties.

I remember getting a pair of new shoes for my birthday on September 27, 1942, which was celebrated at the university. This was the last pair of shoes I wore until after the war.

Of course, we still had to go to school. Marge Cleland and I were put in one age group even though we were one grade apart. Margie did better than I did in math, because Dad was our teacher in addition to running the commissary. Mother taught English, and Mrs. Judge taught us history and geography. She really loved the Peloponnesian Wars and regaled us with the tale of the three hundred Spartans and the Battle of Thermopylae.

The British and Americans were separated into two groups. At seven o'clock every morning, we had to line up outside our building in the two national groups for morning roll call. An officer would call out "Huski, Banugh!" which meant "Attention, Count off!" The British would count off in such a way that their numbers were completely incomprehensible. The camp commander, who spoke some English, would make them count off several times, much to the amusement of the rest of us. Sometimes, a small child was passed down behind our backs so as to confuse the count. Roll call could take almost an hour sometimes. We would line up in a column of two with the person in front calling out our number. One morning, Bobsie Rigby called out the number and completely fouled it up. He quickly yelled "Huski, Banugh!" at the commandant, which led to his confusion while the rest of us were trying not to laugh out loud.

Before the war, Auntie Mabel would send us the Caldecott and Newberry Award-winning books. She would also send us the children's books that were runners-up. She sent us the Sunday funnies from the *Los Angeles Times* and the *Examiner* each month. It was a great day when the funnies arrived. We, and all of our friends, would flop down on the floor and become fully engrossed for hours. Those were the days of *Lil Abner, Dick Tracy, Prince Valiant, Flash Gordon, Buck Rogers, The Katzenjammer Kids, Gasoline Alley, Terry and the Pirates, Maggie and Jigs, Little Orphan Annie, The Phantom, Tarzan, Nancy, Alley Oop*, and many, many more. Bill, Pam, and I loved to read. Mother and Dad must have had at least five thousand books in the house not counting our collections of *Big Little Books*. (*Big Little Books* were small, square books with printing on one side and the illustration on the other.)

The university was right next door to our last home. One day, the Japanese drove several large trucks into our driveway. Soldiers entered the house and began taking bushel baskets of our books; made a large pile of them in our front yard, and then set the pile on fire. They then began carrying out our furniture and carpets and loading them on their trucks. We had several large and expensive carpets, which were handmade in China. Mother and Dad watched it all from the upper balcony of the main university building. They had collected that furniture for years. According to Raphael, our manservant, whom Dad met surreptitiously at the common artesian well, the Japs took seven truckloads of our furniture, worth many thousands of pesos (equivalent to fifty cents US) and shipped it all to Japan. Our furniture was Spanish camagon inlaid with ivory. We had two sets of dining room furniture, dining room tables, side boys, and end tables made of red and black nara or camagon wood. Nara is a very heavy and hard wood. Our furniture was purported to be over three hundred years old. A Spanish family, in need of money, would sell off, through an agent, a few pieces of furniture at a time. Mother and Dad would have the pieces stripped and refinished. Our furniture was sought after all throughout the Orient.

Unfortunately, we weren't the only families that lost all of their possessions. Many treasured and irreplaceable family items and valuable things were immediately loaded on Japanese ships to be shipped to Japan. Many of these items were lost at sea due to the accuracy of American submarine torpedoes. Natives were allowed to strip what was left of the homes after the Japs took what they wanted.

Life took on a routine. We awoke each day expecting to be liberated. Don Bell, the voice of the Philippines before Bataan and Corregidor fell, one day reported that an American armada had been sighted with ships as far as the eye could see. Unfortunately, this was all just a fantasy. As the days turned into weeks, which turned into months, it became apparent that the war was not going to be over quickly, and we were all in for the long haul. Japanese airplanes would sometimes make fake bombing runs over our camp and then return later to show their bucktooth grins at us. There were 150 of us interned now, including the British contingent. Sometimes our friends from neutral countries would try to visit us, but the Japanese forbid it. Often, a Japanese officer would ride a horse around the camp just to gloat over us. We kids would picture him as a small monkey riding the back of a dog like some old-time comedy.

On October 13, 1942, we were transferred from the university to the Cebu Club Filipino, which once was a golf and tennis club. (I played there with my friends Louis Aboitiz, Wendell Cutting, and Doug Dou, when I visited Cebu in 1984.) My family occupied a room at the far end of the main building. The club had indoor plumbing and showers, so we bid a not so fond farewell to those hated outhouses. Adults quickly took up the routines of cooking, washing, and teaching school. Our parents were not going to allow us to be illiterate even if we were in a concentration camp. We met several Norwegian sailors already interned at the club, and we all stayed together until the end of the war.

We had our first successful escape while we were at the country club. Frank Hamlin escaped during the night of December 7, 1942. He was a most unlikely escapee. He was a forty-year-old bachelor and self-described "Mama's boy." He looked like a walking skeleton. His mother, on the other hand, was big, fat, and loud. He just climbed the fence and was gone. The guards put up a frantic search but to no avail. His mother survived the war, and, when she was liberated, who should come marching in with a band of Filipino guerillas but her son, looking just as skeletal as when he had escaped.

Another exciting event occurred during our stay at the club: we had a locust swarm. The sky darkened with flying insects, which covered every surface as they ate all of the vegetation in sight. Birds and chickens would sometimes eat so many locusts that their stomachs would burst. If just the abdomen is fried in deep fat, it makes a pretty tasty meal. The swarm lasted for many hours. A couple of Jap planes tried to take off during the swarm and quickly crashed, killing everyone aboard. We were thrilled. The airport was right next to the club, and we heard everything. The Jap garrison was understandably not happy with our conduct, and there was much shouting at us in Japanese.

Throughout the war, Dad was never in good health. He always had high blood pressure. Before the war, Dr. Ramos came to the house on occasion and "bled" him using leeches. Sometimes we did not know if he was going to pull through when he fell ill.

Dad was called in to Japanese headquarters several times for questioning. Cy Padgett, a Filipino, and Dad would be placed in different rooms and questioned for hours on end. The Japs would ask them all the same questions. Dad and Cy were never physically harmed, but the Japs would routinely beat the hell out of the Filipino.

We had not been treated too badly at this point. We had enough food, had books to read from the club library, and occupied ourselves with many diversions: chess tournaments, cribbage tournaments, (which I almost won), bridge tournaments, and any other kind of entertainment we could think up. At the club, I was barefoot most of the time and contracted the worst case of athlete's foot that I ever had. I never really got rid of it until after the war.

As Americans, we were not afraid of being taken out and shot, but we soon realized that we had no status whatsoever with the Japanese Army. The Japs did not look kindly on prisoners of any kind. We were a nuisance.

The friends we had before the war became closer friends as the war dragged on. Hard as it was to believe, our internment usually brought out the best in everyone. If a person was an absolute jerk, however, being penned up like we were made all character flaws that much more glaring. I can remember my father slapping open handed one such character for disrespecting my mother. As kids, we quickly learned that bratty behavior would not be condoned or tolerated.

While we were interned at the club, Bill, Pam, and I converted to Catholicism. Mother had always been Catholic. Dad was ambivalent toward religion, which might have had something to do with his upbringing in a home with a father who was a Protestant preacher. Dad had a lot of friends who were Catholic priests, and they had a standing invitation to join us for Christmas and Thanksgiving dinners and also to celebrate St. Patrick's Day. Dad tried to follow our beliefs, but he could not accept the dogma of the infallibility of the pope, and eventually became an Episcopalian. We had attended Mass on and off for several years, but we had never truly converted. In Montalongon, we walked to Mass every Sunday, which was quite a walk. At the club, we were baptized and had our first confessions all on the same day.

I studied and became an altar boy and served in many, many Masses during the war and after the war until I was in my late twenties. For some reason, the priests would not let anyone in their teens become altar boys, and Bill was denied that duty. He was sorely disappointed. I can still repeat the litany in Latin. Altar boys knelt all through the Mass, rang the bells at the appropriate times, and said the Confiteor aloud.

The Catholic Church today has changed so much from my altar boy days and not always for the better. I still enjoy the Latin Mass, and I have a hard time accepting laypersons giving Communion and drinking from the priest's chalice. In my day, we were not allowed to touch the chalice unless we were priests. I do like the singing during a folk Mass, and I like that the priest faces the congregation during Mass.

On October 14, 1942, we left the club for good although, at that time, none of us then knew that since none of us spoke Japanese. All dates noted in my memoirs are courtesy of Jane Doner's notebook on her Cebu experiences. Jane is one of my friends, a former babysitter, and is several years older than I am.

Pam's Story

The jail was crowded. Women and children slept in one area while men and boys slept in another. I don't have much of a memory for the accommodations or the food. What I do remember vividly was taking a bath. The bathrooms were large open areas with huge cement tubs filled with water set in the center of the floor. We would climb into the tub to take a bath. The tubs were so big they could hold several people at a time. What was memorable was having the Japanese soldiers watching us bathe. I was particularly offended at the Japanese soldiers who watched the young women naked in the bath.

My brother Bill reminded me that one woman was always assigned to watch during the night. As the Japanese soldiers strolled through the room and past the beds of the sleeping women, she was to scream if a soldier approached someone or looked as if he was going to rape one of the women. This was a constant, never-ending fear.

The Japanese looked for men who might have had any connection with the military. They were taken away from their families and housed separately until the time came when they were shipped out to Japan and prison camps there. We learned later that these men were chained on the deck of a Japanese troop ship that was torpedoed by the Allies and sank.[7]

The junior college was a multistory building of either brick or cement brick.[8] I recall that the bathing facilities were in a small building separated from the main college building. This little building housed toilets as well as a single gang shower. There were separate facilities for men and women. This was my first experience at taking a bath in front of other women. At first I tried to take a shower wearing my underpants as I was so uncomfortable undressing in front of others, but my mother teased me so badly I eventually abandoned my underpants and bathed in the nude like everyone else.

The chemistry and biology laboratories still contained all their equipment. Large beakers were in the chemistry classroom, and stuffed animals were still in the biology classroom. The upstairs classrooms were where we had our beds.

When we were in the junior college, I developed three tropical ulcers on my right shin. How they got there, I have no idea, but they were large and festering. Mother tried to clear them up, but all she had was soap. Auntie Billie (Rebecca Self, a retired army nurse) found some medicine that she applied, and they eventually cleared up. The scars were large and visible for many years.

I don't remember much about going to school either in the junior college or later at the Fillipino Club, but my brother Bill remembers that Mrs. Judge (her husband was a judge, but we found it difficult to pronounce his name, Wislizenus, so we called him Judge, and she became Mrs. Judge), Mrs. Doner (Jane Doner's mother—Jane Doner was the oldest girl in our little group of American children), and Dr. Marsden (a geologist) were some of our teachers.

My brother Bob recalls that, "The only teachers I remember were Mrs. Judge, who taught Marge and me history; Dad taught math, and Mother taught English. Marge was a year older than me. Her sister, Mary Lou, was in my brother Bill's grade at school."

Bob says that Dad ran the storeroom, where one could buy cigarettes and other goodies. Mother worked in the kitchen. I, of course, have no recollection of what our parents were doing at that time, being completely absorbed with my own affairs.

I do remember Father Gries, a Roman Catholic missionary priest from Belgium, who gave my brothers and me our catechism lessons in preparation for baptism in the Catholic faith. At the same time, my father was taking instructions from Father William McCarthy, the Maryknoll missionary who had blessed my parents' marriage. (Neither Father Gries nor Father McCarthy are mentioned in the letter by Lucy Brown listing the Internees at the Junior College.) Our father never became a Catholic, as he could not accept the dogma of the infallibility of the pope. He did, however, receive instructions and did eventually become baptized an Episcopalian. As he said, this was as close as he could come to being a Catholic. I have found a letter of his to his sister Hazel, who was asking advice about a friendship she was having with a Catholic man. My father wrote, "If I can marry one, you can talk to one." There was a strong prejudice against Catholics in my father's family.

For some reason, and I have no idea why, we children decided to train for the army. My brother Bill was the general or captain; I don't really remember what rank he conferred upon himself. Marge and I were lowly privates. One of our duties was to patrol the perimeter of the college building after dark in the evening. I am not sure what we used for rifles but something like a long stick, I am sure. One evening, I was assigned guard duty first and began my trip around the building fairly bravely until I got to the darkest part, where there were no lights, and I heard rustling in the bushes. I ran all the way back to the main steps. I was always afraid of the dark. I found to my shame that the rustling was caused by my brother Bill observing my behavior as a guard on patrol. He announced to everyone that I had failed in my duty.

One day, we all gathered at a safe distance from the fence that enclosed the college (getting too near the fence or camp perimeter was to expose oneself to the possibility of being shot) to watch Japanese soldiers carrying our furniture, books, and clothing out of our house.

The furniture, glassware, and China, we were told, were to be taken to Japan. It was Mother's custom to buy furniture and china whenever we traveled, and we had some lovely pieces from Japan and China as well as the Philippines. The books and clothing were piled in the yard and set on fire. We could have used those clothes, as we had so little with us, and the books would have rounded out the few that were in camp.

Before the occupation, we had an extensive library, most of which had been sent to us by my mother's sister, Mabel Rice. At that time, Auntie Mabel was teaching children's literature and writing extensively, so had access to review copies of new books. Some, like the Tom Mix books, were signed by the author. To stand helplessly by and watch all our possessions either being carted away or set on fire made us realize that our lives had changed unalterably and forever. Later, we found individual pieces of our silverware that had been buried on the college grounds. We ended up with one or two pieces, and I am sure others found whatever else was left. Since we had to provide our own dishes, flatware, and glasses for meals, anything we could find was used.

Every morning we all collected in front of the main building for roll call. We were placed in two lines and counted off to see if anyone had escaped during the night. When the camp commandant arrived, we were to bow to him to show respect. We were not very good at bowing correctly, and our guards became quite frustrated in their attempts to teach us. It was one of our small pleasures that we never did learn to bow correctly. We were quite deliberate in our efforts to see who could frustrate the guards the most.

We were also unable to learn Japanese, although the guards tried very hard to teach us their language. My father never acknowledged that he understood them very well.

When we outgrew the junior college, we were relocated to the Fillipino Club.

The Fillipino Club was the country club and social center for Cebu expatriates before the war. It consisted of a golf course, an upstairs ballroom with a bar, shower facilities, and kitchen. The club probably had tennis courts as well, as I recall my father was a competitive tennis player. We slept upstairs in the ballroom, with women in one area, men in another. The sleeping areas were separated by a single wall of blankets.

My brothers and I were baptized into the Catholic faith on December 8, 1942, while we were still at the Fillipino Club. Father William McCarthy heard our first confessions and baptized us just before Mass. Auntie Billie, one of our sponsors in baptism, made us little pillows to kneel on as baptismal gifts. Mass was celebrated in an area used for a variety of activities, so we knelt on the bare cement floor.

Evidently, we obtained and prepared our own breakfasts, as I have a vague memory of Father McCarthy thanking Mother for a breakfast she had prepared for all of us and had invited him to share.

I have a very vivid memory of the day the locusts came. They arrived suddenly. The sky simply turned black. I watched as people ran around collecting them in butterfly nets, then building a fire and roasting the locusts over the fire. Although I watched in disgust, I had no trouble tasting one when someone offered it to me. I found roasted locust to be a delicious food and ate as many as I could get.

During the locust invasion, one incident gave us great pleasure. A small airplane took off from a nearby area. As it tried to lift off the ground, its engine became clogged with locusts and crashed. Since we assumed the plane was piloted by Japanese and carried soldiers, we cheered and laughed and danced.

It was at the Fillipino Club that I first became aware of guerrillas. One morning, the camp was buzzing with whispers, and everyone was warned not to say anything out loud for fear our guards would hear. A young man had escaped during the night, and it was said he had joined the guerrillas. We did not want the guards to know whose son he was in case they decided to torture his mother to find out where he had been planning to go. We were all warned by our camp leaders never to talk about this incident to protect her. I never heard whether or not he had been recaptured, but I hoped he had gotten away safely.

Chapter 6

LIFE ABOARD A JAPANESE TROOP SHIP

Bill's Notes

Our next instructions, around December 1942, were, "Take warm clothes and pack. You are being transferred." We thought we were headed for Formosa.

We did pack. We were taken by truck to the docks and loaded on a freighter. Our quarters were rat-infested, low-plank decking in the hold.

Our toilet was a planked wood lean-to our men had to build over the side of the ship. Our meals were maggoty rice. We shared our quarters with Japanese infantry.

At Bohol, we stopped to pick up soldiers and more civilian prisoners. I have no recollection of the trip's duration.

I vividly remember passing south of Corregidor. Burned, darkened, barren with caves dark, and the whole effect that of a skull staring at us.

Yes, we were transferred to Santo Thomas and later to Los Baños prison camps.

Bob's Notes

We were taken by trucks to Cebu Harbor. There we were met with the sight of a small, dirty, Japanese tramp freighter. There were no accommodations for us. After we boarded the ship, we were put in the cargo hold. The hold had wooden shelves that we slept on and an open space in the middle where we made "camp." And, to our shock, half the hold was already taken up by Japanese soldiers. There was a one-hole latrine that hung off the port side of the ship. We eventually got the Japs to put a curtain up for modesty. Being a male had its advantages, since we could do some of our business over the side while carefully watching which direction the wind was blowing.

Luckily, we were able to stay topside most of the time. Sleeping was very hard, and the soldiers were no better off than we were. There was no way to bathe, so it got very pungent after dark when we slept in the hold (well, attempted to sleep). Everyone shared the same food. Thankfully, there were no incidents of poor behavior from the soldiers toward us. It was a slow, tedious, and dirty trip. It seemed that our three-hundred-mile trip could be literally measured in inches.

Pam's Notes

Eventually, there were too many of us to be housed at the Fillipino Club, and we were to be sent to Manila, where there was a large university that had been converted into an internment camp. Civilian Allies from all over the islands were being rounded up and brought to Santo Tomas University in Manila. There was no other way to transport all of us from Cebu City on the island of Cebu, which is in the center of the island chain, to Manila on the island of Luzon in the north, other than by ship.

Our ship was a tramp steamer. It was unprepossessing and dirty. Bill told me that since it was a troop ship, there was a barrier in the hold with the women and children on one side and the soldiers on the other. They would look over the barrier to watch us. During the day, the roof of the hold was left open, and at night, it was closed.

We were warned not to leave the hold without permission, so we ate, slept, and socialized there for the week we were on board. We were allowed to go up on deck periodically when our guards felt it was safe to do so.

One woman created a shower stall for herself by putting up blankets all around. She took a bath on deck with the Japanese standing around watching her. My mother said the woman had decided she could not tolerate not having a bath, and anything was worth getting clean again. Bill told me that Margery Cleland got a bucket of water to bathe in the hold. She was unaware, apparently, that while she was taking a bath, the guards were watching her over the barrier.

The Japanese are known for their love and care for children, and our guards tried to make life as bearable as possible for us, bringing us rock candy or extra rations of hardtack. These gifts did not diminish our fear of them but were gratefully received nevertheless

We arrived in Manila and were transported from the ship to the Santo Tomas University, where all the prisoners were held.

Chapter 7

SANTO TOMAS INTERNMENT CAMP

Bill's Story

Landing at Manila harbor, we were transferred by truck to Santo Tomas University. The entrance was tree lined and very attractive. Immediately, Mother and Pam were assigned to a room in the main building. Dad, Bob, and I were sent to the gym. It was a huge room filled with row upon row of bunks. (There are pictures on the Internet of the interior of the gym with its rows of beds.) Later, we were thankful to be transferred. For a while, Dad, Bob, and I were assigned to a room next to the one Mother and Pam were in. Again, we were transferred. This time to the education building: Bob and I to a former scouter, Mr. Lesk; Dad to the first floor.

Santo Tomas was our home and school for another year. A place for teenagers to grow but not under nourishing conditions. I know I had a bout of dysentery. New POWs coming up from Mindanao had contracted typhus in their freighter.

I remember getting a Red Cross delivery. The cigarettes had the slogan: "And slap the Japs" on them. We had to remove the packages from the boxes. I helped, and, of course, smoked the cigarettes.

During this period, one group of internees was chosen to be repatriated. We watched them leave with mixed emotions.

Bob's Story

On October 19, 1942, we arrived at our destination: Manila harbor. It was a good thing we didn't know where we going when we boarded the ship, but it really wouldn't have made any difference anyway. Manila had been called the "Pearl of the Orient." MacArthur had declared Manila an "open city" to spare it from any destruction by invading troops. This was my first time there, and, even if it was the largest city in the Philippines, I had no interest in sightseeing.

After we docked, we were loaded onto trucks and driven through the city. We kept our eyes front and did not look around. We were very worried about where we were going and what awaited us once we got there. As we traveled, the streets were eerily quiet. There were no cries of "Americanos" that we had become so used to hearing.

Our final destination was the University of Santo Tomas, which was high-walled and completely fenced. As we drove through the main campus, we passed nipa structure guard barracks on our approach to the main or administration building. Here was where most of the women, girls, and young boys were housed. The hundreds of men and older boys, Bill and I included, were housed in the gym. There was row upon row of cots on the gymnasium floor, including some in the bleachers. Each cot was a foot apart from the next one.

Later on, we transferred into the education building, which was adjacent to the main. Dad was housed on the first floor, while Bill and I occupied different rooms on the third floor. There were fifteen boys to a room. Bill bunked with the high school boys, while I shared a room with other boys my age except one high school senior, Paul, who enjoyed beating me up. I could outbox his little brother, who was my age, but Paul would always whale on me for beating up his brother when I came back to the third floor. Paul's bullying ended when he met the end of my two-by-four. Our room group was called "Mr. Leek's Boys" but I never saw Mr. Leek do anything except for the one time he found me beating the stuffing out of one of my roommates, David, and he eventually broke up the fight. Unfortunately, David's mother was my history teacher, and I bore the brunt of her extra homework for months.

There was a very well-stocked library on our floor that contained the complete works of Edgar Rice Burroughs and Horatio Alger, as well as the *Hardy Boys*. I happily read all of the *Tarzan*, *Bomba*, and *The Jungle Boy* books before we were transferred once again. There was never a chance to read the *Hardy Boys* and *Tom Swift*. We also had access to a complete set of encyclopedias, which was a treasure trove of reading for a young boy. The Japanese had not seen fit to destroy the biology books or the botany displays, so we had textbooks to aid in our studies. I used to read until it was too dark to see, and I still tried anyway.

My internment camp education helped me tremendously after we were liberated. I hardly ever needed to pick up an English or history textbook in high school. Math, on the other hand, was still a disaster. I barely passed Algebra I and II and Plane Geometry. I did have to read my Spanish textbook because our teacher, Mrs. Johnson, pushed us very hard.

School was one way for us to pass the time at Santos Tomas. I was still in the sixth grade, but now my classes were very large. Except for classes in the States, I had never been in a class with more than four students. I used a "one-armed" desk for the first time. I don't remember any of my teachers except for an Englishwoman who made a lasting impression on me. She really liked the "Rhyme of the Ancient Mariner," and she wielded a mean yardstick. Jimmy Fisher got hit a lot. We called her Miss "Abbath but Rock." We followed the same school schedule that we had in Cebu: school from eight to twelve, then lunch, siesta time, and then free for the rest of the afternoon.

There was every kind of field game available. We had several basketball courts, football and soccer fields, baseball diamonds, and boxing rings. Even with a large British contingent, no one ever played cricket. I learned how to play soccer, and I excelled at kicking and dribbling the ball barefooted. I had never even heard of basketball. Thanks to Jack Padgett, I had learned how to play football with very silly rules. I learned to play it right in Santo Tomas. The two hardest things for me to learn were how to dribble a basketball and how to throw a football. The softball diamonds were on the right of the main street, and the basketball courts were on the left. We were allowed to trade with the native Filipinos for the sports equipment we needed.

Boxing contests were held regularly, and age divisions were set up. The older boys' bouts were pretty brutal. They could really knock each other out. This was the first time I had gone to school with Mestizos (white father and Filipino mother) and black Americans. Black fathers had been soldiers in the Philippines.

I learned the childhood games of marbles and mumblety-peg. I got pretty good at marbles, but I could never beat one little marble player who always seemed to win most of the marbles in camp. We always played mumblety-peg barefooted.

One other activity we thoroughly enjoyed was not found on a field. We liked to spy on the high school kids, especially when they were dating. That was an education we would never find in a book.

Mealtime was a time that we could be together as a family. Food was served at the rear of the main building, and everyone was issued a mess card that was punched when we were served. They did not want anyone going back for seconds. Meals were served twice a day, at 7:00 a.m. and at 5:00 p.m. Four long lines would form at the sound of the meal bell. In the morning, there was rice and coffee (no coffee for the young kids). Little kids got milk, and we preteenagers got nothing because we were at that awkward age between "baby food" and "adult food." In the evening, there was a ladle of rice or, hopefully, a ladle of stew with the meat well concealed. Everybody had a large tin can that was fitted with wire handles to hold our meager meals. Although the food wasn't tasty, it was ample in those early war years, and, thankfully, no one went hungry.

There was an adequate hospital on campus, which was manned by civilian doctors and the army and navy nurses who had been captured in Bataan and Corregidor. Dengue fever, malaria, and amoebic and bacillary dysentery were the most common ailments. Tropical fevers, which were as hard to cure as the common cold, were a frequent ailment.

Mother and Dad obtained a couple of camp chairs, and, in the evening, we would meet them outside the education building. We entertained ourselves with camp shows we called the "Theater under the Stars." The Japanese would sometimes even show us a war movie, but when it got to the part when the "enemy" (us) were attacking the "good guys" (them), we internees would start clapping and whistling, and the show was over.

A buddy and I once observed, through the guards' fence, some natives being water-tortured as punishment for coming into camp and trying to steal from the internees. The Japs thought they were spies. We stopped watching when they started raising their Samurai swords over the captives' necks.

If an internee ever tried to escape and was subsequently caught, he was forced to dig his own grave and then shot, falling into the hole. Several internees tried to escape, and there were many graves to mark their failure.

None of the boys or younger men wore shirts, and that was fine by me. I only owned two shirts: one for Mass and another that Mother had knitted from string. Our shoes began to wear out, and we either went barefoot or wore a wooden sandal called a *bakya*.

We had some enterprising street vendors in camp that sold goodies to the other internees. I especially remember the taffy man and the guy who would just sell fresh ground peanut butter. Bill began selling sweet rolls. A friend and I tried to go into the shoeshine business (two-color golf shoes were the hardest), but it was ultimately doomed to fail, since not a lot of us had shoes. We, stupidly, set up our shoeshine stand right next to one run by two Americans: one was a black former professional boxer before the war. He and I got into an argument one day, and he hit me in the groin, which caused me to urinate all over myself. He obviously had no conscience in beating up a twelve-year-old. I never told Dad because I was afraid he might take the guy on. I never went around that place again if I could help it. My partner eventually tried to cheat me out of my share of the profits, and we angrily parted company. He and I used to spar a lot, and he never liked being hit in the face. That ended after he cheated me, and he got one right in the kisser.

It was possible to have small nipa shacks built for a family. Our shanty consisted of one elevated room with *sawali* walls and bamboo slatted floors. The shanties enabled the families to be together and allowed the parents a little privacy. We lived in an area of the camp called "Froggy Bottom." Names for some of the other areas were "Out Yonder," "Glamour Ville," "Southwest Territory," "Shanty Town," "Garden Court Extension," "Jungle Town," "Father's Garden," "Jerkville," and "Dead End." The shanty on one side of us was occupied by a black husband and an American Indian wife who really had some knockdown drag-out fights. There was always yelling and screaming, but sometimes she also threw pots and pans. She once threw a butcher knife that stuck in the post next to his head. A bachelor lived on our other side in the smallest shanty in camp. He was just happy to be out of the gym. We had a little charcoal brazier to cook with, and, when the meal was over, the dirty dishes were loaded into a tin wash basin and carried to the washing troughs at the rear of the education building. I used to hate having to do those dishes. Dad and I would get into shouting matches over them. One night Mother asked me to do the dishes, and I sassed her back. My dad immediately knocked me down and said, "You can't talk to my wife like that." Funny, I had never considered her to be his wife until that time. I always thought of her as my mother. Needless to say, I did the dishes that night and every night afterward when it was my turn.

I was not interested in girls at this stage of my life. Sometimes girls had interest in me, but that was their problem. I had friends who were girls, and some of my best friends were Betty Padgett and Margie Cleland, but not as girlfriends. I didn't reach puberty until way after the war, which was good because when I hit it, I hit it with a vengeance. We had dances and really enjoyed the square dances because we did not have to hold a girl for too long. I enjoyed the Virginia reel, an Irish/Scottish folk dance dating back to the seventeenth century, the most.

We had several characters in camp. Ovid Bonney, who was very good on the violin, was a fully mature man at the age of twelve. He had a dark beard, receding hairline, was hairy all over, and probably not over five feet tall. He suffered from a childhood disease that quickly ages children and they, unfortunately, have an abbreviated life span. When his brother, David, introduced him to me, I thought Ovid was David's father. Howard Hawks was another standout. There was really nothing unusual about him except that he was six foot six inches tall, which made him the tallest man in camp. Sailor was someone I always felt a little sorry for. Sailor had been a professional boxer and was punch-drunk. He could hardly speak and could not stand still at all. He had very poor balance and was constantly in motion. I heard that in his day he was quite a fighter but never figured out when to hang up his gloves.

We also had prostitutes, which I, at the time, knew very little about. Some of them were very nice and helped out where they could. I remember one who thought she was pregnant but had a tumor instead and died soon after.

Priests, nuns, and missionaries, along with their families, were not required to be interned while we were at Santos Tomas. They would learn of our harsh camp life during the last year of the war when we all moved to Los Baños.

Life goes on regardless of the circumstances. There were some marriages during our stay at Santos Tomas. One of my old teachers, who really was rather young, fell in love and got married. There were several births. There were many deaths from disease, old age, and from our captors.

On September 26, 1943, all of the 127 Allied consular staff members were allowed to leave camp, aboard the *Teia Maru,* and sent to Goa, a Portuguese colony in India, where they were exchanged with POWs from China and other parts of the Orient who had left Goa on the *Gripsholm*. We were very happy for the repatriated consular staff and wished them well. (See the letter from Lucy Brown sent from Lourengo Marques, Portuguese East Africa, to my aunt, Mabel F. Rice. The letter was meant to be copied and sent to the relatives of all the internees mentioned in the letter. She and her husband, Ack Brown, left Cebu on June 13, 1942, on a British-Japanese diplomatic exchange, as Ack was British vice consul in Davao. Her letter is in the appendix.)

We received our first care package from the Dutch Red Cross soon after the *Teia Maru* left. I guess the Japs wanted the world to know just how kind they were to us. The package was small and contained a few food items that we were deprived of: coffee, canned powdered milk, canned cheese, and corned beef. In total, we received three care packages: two from the Dutch Red Cross and one from the USA. The Japs loved the American care packages because they not only contained all kinds of food but also included cigarettes. They confiscated everything of value to them, which left us with very little food. We also received a different parcel containing clothes and Keds tennis shoes. These three care packages would be the only ones we would ever receive during our three-and-a-half-year internment.

During the monsoon season of 1943, there was so much rain that the camp drains could not funnel off any more water, and the campus started flooding. Santo Tomas was surrounded with walls that acted like the sides of a bathtub, and the water level eventually reached knee level. Food was floated from one building to another. For us seventh-graders, it was a lot of fun. We didn't mind the warm rain, and we had many happy games of water football. After the water finally abated, we found a lot of fish in the canals around the camp, which improved our diets immensely.

***

Pam's Story

We Cebuanos were transported by truck from our ship to the University of Santo Tomas Internment Camp. We were now called internees to distinguish us from military men captured at the fall of Bataan and Corregidor, who were in a prisoner of war camp. We were treated differently, too.

"Late Saturday afternoon, December 19, 1943 most of the camp gathered around the Commandant's Office to await the arrival of the 146 people who had been interned in Cebu." (Hartendorp, 99.)

Mother and I were assigned to a large classroom on the third floor of the main building for our sleeping quarters. Dad and my brothers were assigned to the gym.

Not long after we arrived, the Japanese began freeing the Swiss and Swedish prisoners, as they were neutrals. The Swedish sailors who had been jailed with us in Cebu refused to leave and remained in camp with the rest of us. Our Swiss friends, the Goebbels, were released, and spent the rest of the war in Manila city. (Lucy Goebels told me she was writing her memoirs about life in Manila during the war, but I have found no evidence that she published it or even if she finished it before she died of cancer.)

Santo Tomas was a large, open playground for children. Other than school, we were largely unsupervised and wandered the camp at will. Surprisingly, we didn't get into any serious trouble. This was such a marked change from our lives before the war, when we were under the constant supervision of the family servants and amahs.

A group of us loved to play with knives. We would draw a circle in the dirt and throw knives to the ground to see which one was the closest to the center. We broke a lot of knives that way, so to replace them, we would climb up to look in the window of the lost and found office, which was on the ground floor of the main building, memorize what a particular knife looked like, then would go into the office and describe the knife, claiming it as our own.

We also played marbles. We would draw a circle in the dirt and each of us would put in our allotment of marbles. Then from outside the circle we would try to get our marble to strike another marble and make it run out of the ring. The winner was the one who collected the most marbles. We got our marble supply the same place we got our knives.

One day the men had an army-navy football game. It was a great game. I rooted for navy. I think they lost.

There was a large open area in front of the main building that was used by the Japanese to show full-length propaganda movies to the entire camp. People would bring folding chairs and stools to sit on, or blankets, and we children sat on the ground and usually fell asleep before the movie was over. Other times there were different internee entertainments. One that impressed me for a long time was an artist who created pictures with long sweeping movements of his arm. I tried to emulate his methods but was singularly unsuccessful. In the evenings, we also would gather to sing the favorite songs we all knew. Since radios were forbidden in the camps for fear we would receive news of the war, we were on our own for entertainment.

Every able-bodied adult in camp had an assigned job. Those who could teach were assigned to teach the children, creating lessons as best they could, either from recall or the available books. Classes were offered not just for the grade-school children but high school and college as well. People donated the books they had brought to the camp to be used as a lending library in addition to the books that still remained in the university library. Food was distributed by the central kitchen twice a day, and we stood in line with our dishes to receive our portion—mostly rice. Others were assigned latrine cleanup, or garbage collection, as well as policing. One of my friends wanted to grow up and be a garbage collector just like his dad. We children had no concept of liberation and simply accepted that this is where we were going to live for the rest of our lives.

Apparently, it wasn't just the children who expected to live the rest of their lives in the prison camp. I had an English boyfriend. We were inseparable and vowed to be faithful forever. I believe we were ten years old at the time. His mother broke up our relationship by forbidding him to play with me. She was afraid we would grow up and marry. They were Church of England while we were Catholic. It's funny looking back on it now, but at the time, I was devastated.

I vividly recall being frightened of an impending history exam, so much so that I literally worried myself sick and ended up in the camp hospital with intractable diarrhea. Mother had made me some diapers out of a blanket so that I would not mess myself. At the hospital, there was no toilet paper, and I asked everyone who came to see me to bring me some, as I was having a great deal of trouble "holding it in." Toilet paper was in short supply, so asking the other patients for some resulted in nothing at all. I was in the bed next to Margie Cleland, but I have no idea why she was hospitalized. When I finally got back to our dormitory, Mother took me to the shower and scrubbed my bottom with soap, in cold water, until she could remove all the dried feces I had accumulated. That was the most painful bath I have ever had.

The camp hospital was a two-storied building staffed by physicians and the army and navy nurses who had been left behind on Corregidor and Bataan. I was on the second floor. The hospital ward was one large room with three rows of iron cots with a table or bedside table between the cots. (There is a good photograph of the hospital ward on the Internet with the rest of the photographs of the Santo Tomas camp.) There was no privacy between the beds. There was one toilet with a limited number of toilet stools.

My best friends in Santo Tomas were Marcia Newlin and Roxanna Goodier. Roxanna and her mother were in the same dormitory room with Mother and me. I admired Roxanna's little gold stud earrings. I pleaded for a pair and never understood that the money we had went into food and clothes, and could not be given to a little girl's heart's desire.

Because we all slept and lived closely together, infectious diseases and parasites were transmitted rapidly. While in Santo Tomas, I became infested with head lice. The treatment was to soak the entire head in kerosene and wrap it up tightly in a towel. Since Mother and I slept in the same bed, she was not interested in getting lice too. I was unlucky enough also to have chicken pox at the same time; so the kerosene treatment on the open sores on my head was agony.

Bobsie Rigby's mother, Grace, died of cancer while we were in Santo Tomas. Bobsie was a good friend from my class in Cebu, and his mother had been our third-grade teacher. She was a lovely woman. This was my first experience with death. I was told that Bobsie and his father were allowed to leave camp for her burial in the Catholic cemetery. I was also told that it was raining that day, and the empty grave was half filled with water. Whether or not I was told this to frighten me, I have no idea, but the image has stayed with me.

Bobsie talked my brother Bob into becoming an altar boy. Although my brother Bill wanted to be an altar boy, he was told that he was too old. Pre-Vatican II rules did not always make sense.

In the main building, the doors had been torn off the women's toilets. A few women made curtains for the toilet stalls to provide some privacy. One day, some of the older girls decided to play a trick on the women and shut all the curtains, signifying that the toilet was in use. The line got very long. Some friends and I got down on the floor and looked for feet below the curtain. If we could see no feet, we would announce that the toilet was empty.

When toilet paper ran out and *The Light that Failed*, a novel we used for toilet paper, also ran out, we used cloths that we carried around that had to be washed between uses. That was Mother's job.

I was told of a seven-year-old girl who had died. Her mother was so overcome with grief she wanted to put her in a coffin with a glass lid so she could keep her close. Another child was a blue baby, born with a heart defect. With the onset of the war, his family had been unable to take him to the States for surgery. He was a plucky little boy, walking along slowly, squatting every few steps or so to catch his breath. He died in camp.

We had a shanty in "Shanty Town." (See the photographs of Santo Tomas online) It was basically a nipa hut with one open room and a covered porch where there was a hibachi pot for cooking. It was the only place where we, as a family, could gather for some privacy and store some of our items. I remember reading the best bits to Mother from children's books I had borrowed from the library. For my birthday present that year, Mother made me navy bean soup. The hut just behind us housed a Scottish couple with their adorable redheaded two-year-old son, Jamie, who was never dressed in anything but diapers. I thoroughly enjoyed "watching out" for Jamie from time to time.

One day, and for no apparent reason, we were allowed outside the camp in order to attend Mass at what I thought was a cathedral. It was a huge, magnificent church, so large, we children ran all the way down the aisle so we could sit in the front pew.

On another day, there was an excited buzz around the camp. "Red Cross boxes!" Dad and my brothers went to get ours. They were forty-pound boxes of canned and boxed foods. Some women managed to conserve the contents of their boxes until almost the end. My mother was still convinced we would be rescued any day, so she did not conserve as well.

Eventually Santo Tomas became overcrowded with five thousand internees and more expected. The Japanese asked for volunteers to go to another camp that was being prepared at the Los Baños Agricultural College. The navy nurses volunteered to go, leaving the army nurses in charge of the hospital in Santo Tomas. Our family volunteered to go. As it turns out, my father made a very good decision. We missed the shelling of Santo Tomas during the liberation of Manila. (See *The War*, a Ken Burns PBS film on disc 5, or his book with Geoffrey Ward, *The War: An Intimate History, 1941–1945*, 339–46, with photos of the internees.)

Chapter 8

OUR LIVES AT LOS BAÑOS

Bill's Recall

The time came when our family had to leave Santo Tomas. We were selected to transfer to Los Baños on the other side of Laguna de Bay. We left from the front of the main building. We were loaded into trucks. I may have that incorrect. I have no memory of that trip. We may have been in boxcars. I remember waiting to leave. I don't remember arriving in Los Baños.

I do remember nipa-roofed barracks. I recall the small rooms and latrines and showers between the barracks.

We continued schooling until our diet interfered with our vision. No slug was left untouched. We grew okra because it matured quickly though we had to pick it small, otherwise the okra would disappear overnight.

Life went on or ceased. Some died of undulant fever. Bob didn't. Dad came down with severe beriberi. If we had not been rescued by the Eleventh Airborne, Third Cavalry, and guerillas, he would have died in camp. Pat Held was shot returning to camp with fresh produce.

American successes brought renewed cuts in our diet. Finally, we were down to two hundred grams of rice a day.

A Grumman fighter came over on fire. We watched it roll over as the pilot bailed out. He survived and was rescued by a submarine after the guerillas helped him.

We watched F-38s, B-24s and B-25s come over. We knew the war was approaching us. The fighting part, that is.

Bob's Recall

After much consideration and many conversations with Mother, Dad ultimately decided that we should transfer to Los Baños with a large group of other internees. The camp was set up at the Agricultural College, which had been a division of the University of the Philippines before the war. Santo Tomas was getting too full of internees, so many needed to be relocated. Dad had been assured that we would be able to live together as a family there, which would be the first time since we left Cebu.

On April 7, 1944, the whole camp got up at 3:30 a.m. to prepare for the departure of the 530 internees bound for Los Baños. Mrs. Judge, my old kindergarten principal, joined our family for breakfast with the Doners (who would not be joining us) in front of Main third floor room 55-A, where the Doner women lived. Mrs. Judge left camp with the first group at 7:00 a.m. We left with the second group at 2:00 p.m., and before we left, Mrs. Doner cooked a lunch of mongo beans boiled with onions and pepper, scrambled eggs, and coffee. We gave the Doners some things we could not take: charcoal, empty boxes, bottles, and some coconuts. Empty boxes and bottles were useful items to have.

Robin Prising stayed behind at Santo Tomas, and his book, *Manila, Goodbye* chronicles the hardships he faced after we left. All I have to say, after reading his book, was that he sure didn't live the same war that I did.

We traveled south by truck, always accompanied by our ever-vigilant guards, to Los Baños. It was a long, tedious trip. The only highlight was a stop we made to swim in an algae-laden swimming pool with our guards. Not many took advantage of the swim, but Bill and I certainly did. When we arrived at Los Baños, we quickly discovered it was far different from Santo Tomas. The original Los Baños campus consisted of a church, gymnasium, office buildings, and a laboratory, as well as other small buildings, which were occupied by earlier internees. The men who preceded us had built nipa barracks for us that were to be our new homes. We were assigned two and a half rooms in the barracks with a little cook station located under a nipa awning. We quickly cut a door in Bill's and my room and took a wall out of Mother, Dad, and Pam's room to create a larger living space. Close by our rooms was the bathhouse and latrines. We never had anything other than cold water for bathing, which would become a serious problem when we began slowly starving to death.

The Laceys were on one side of our modified rooms, and the Hogebooms were on the other. The Hogebooms were Seventh-Day Adventists and did not eat meat. Whenever we were served stew with any kind of meat in it, they would always give it to us. I had a lot of respect for them, and their children were among the nicest kids in camp. They were as blonde as Bill, Pam, and I.

We were fed two times a day. At first, the food was plentiful and as tasty as can be expected for prisoner food. One of us would take all of our food pails and go to the communal serving line and bring the food back to our family area for consumption. Food was ladled out to waiting internees. The cry of "Hot stuff, coming through!" was a welcome sound. Being a camp cook at the central kitchen was a job to kill for because we always could eat the scraps left over in carts and large pots.

We were allowed to have little garden plots. I grew onions, papayas, peanuts, and *camotes* (sweet potatoes). We also were allowed to take wood-chopping trips outside of the camp.

There was an old chapel that was elevated and had two sloping driveways. David Devries, Tommy Johnson, and I built a go-cart and ran down those driveways and the adjacent sloping street. We stole all of the wood, metal, and rope for our go-cart. We cut wooden wheels from canal covers and plated them with tin. The cart could ride four people: a driver in front and three in the back. We had no problem with kids willing to push us up the chapel hill so that they could get a ride. Our problem was wear and tear. The tin wheel casings would wear out, and the rope, used for binding around the steering wheel, would rot and break at the most inopportune time. Replacements, understandably, became harder and harder to find as the war continued.

I was in the eighth grade now. We went to school in the morning, which left the afternoon free. The junior high kids played the high school kids in both football and soccer. We would have played basketball and baseball, but we had neither the equipment nor the facility.

The Japs insisted that when we encountered a camp guard, we were to bow and show our respect. Although they loathed prisoners on general Japanese principles, they still demanded respect from us. We invented all sorts of ways to avoid bowing to them. Us kids simply ran away, or we would turn our backs on them so we could not see them.

A sawali wall separated us from another section of camp. Nipa barracks, like our own, had been constructed there, and that's where the Japs started housing priests, nuns, and missionaries who had been living outside of the confines of captivity for the last two and a half years. It wasn't until the wall was taken down and the two camps were allowed to become one that we learned that what we called the "Holy City" contained the people who called us "Hell's Half Acre."

The priests and missionaries brought with them some of the children of men who had maintained mistresses before the war: mestizos who were the product of a white father and a native mother. The Japs felt that these kids were Allies and belonged in camp. These children caused their fathers and their families much embarrassment. Most of the fathers had enlisted in the army and had been in a concentration camp not knowing of their existence.

Granddad Cleland and Father George were among the last people to enter Los Baños. They had tried to escape to Australia and had been captured and tortured mercilessly by the Japanese. At one point, they were severely beaten and hung up on a tree for three days before finally being cut down. They were both elderly men but somehow survived. When Granddad came into camp, he claimed his son Morrie's mestizo family as his own. (Mary Lou Cleland Hedrick says that her grandfather, Dad Cleland, was an internee in Santo Tomas. She does not recall that he went to Los Baños.)

Throughout our captivity, the Japanese sent several ships loaded with male POWs bound for Japan. Most of them never made it, as the ships were sunk by our own navy. Most of our friends' mothers found out they were widows at the end of the war.

Starting in the fall of 1944, our two-meal-a-day rations began to be cut down and cut down, and ultimately cut out altogether. Being hungry is a feeling that does not go away. When you are starving, you stay hungry after you eat. That gnawing hunger is constantly with you. All you can think about is food—what your favorite food is, how you like it cooked, and what it was like to eat it. No meal would ever be enough to eat. As our starvation grew, we noticed that even the mosquitoes ignored us. Starvation, strangely, gives you cravings for food you never liked. We kids had always been picky eaters before the war. We would refuse to eat something because we didn't like it, which infuriated Dad.

We were ladled, one scoop per family member, rice mush or corn meal mush with or without bugs (usually weevils) twice a day. We eventually wound up eating *lugao*, a watery rice soup. Sometimes we would receive rice that was only half husked.

We would supplement our rations with anything we could scrounge. We ate the heart of the banana tree (which was inedible), cassava beans (which bloated our stomachs and gave us gas), and fried banana peels (which were good and tasty if we could ever find some). Some people, like Dr. Marsden, ate grubs and worms, but most of us never became that desperate.

Bill and I were able to get jobs in the camp gardens, weeding the plots, digging, and plastering holes to collect rainwater. We were paid one hundred grams of rice a week, which is about the size of a six-ounce tuna can. Mother also got a job in the camp gardens picking seeds out of the vegetables for replanting. We could keep the pulp and eat the remainder. As we were gradually getting less food each day, it became harder to get warm after our cold showers at the end of the day's work. We would have to stand out in the sunlight to get warm. Another side effect of starvation is that when we had to go to the bathroom, we had to go immediately. Often, I had to make a mad dash to the bathroom in the middle of the night. We lived right next to the men's bath area, and the sound of urination into tin urinals would be almost constant throughout the night. My muscles soon began to lose the ability to keep everything in its place.

Dad contracted beriberi, a disease that collects water between the skin tissues and makes people look like they are suffering from elephantiasis. We finally had to take him to the hospital. He had been giving us his rations, saying he was not hungry, and we were so hungry that we pretended not to notice. Dad eventually became so sick that he could no longer walk. Pam fared better than Bill or I. She was a cute little blonde-haired girl who captivated the Japanese soldiers. The Japs would give food to the little children who imitated Japanese soldiers, and Pam occasionally got some handouts. Some of the smallest kids, who had never seen soldiers, would march behind the Japs calling out "hup one, hup two," and they loved that.

I came down with a tropical fever and started to slowly dehydrate to the point that I was put into the hospital. Our nurses were nuns. Bert Fonger, a big, strapping fellow of nineteen, was in the bed next to mine and was suffering with a fever like mine. His temperature got so high that one night he lay on the concrete floor to cool off and caught pneumonia. He died a few days later. Bert was a nice kid and was on the wood-cutting crew. Neither Dad nor I had the strength to visit each other. After I got out of the hospital, I still was very weak, and without an adequate diet, my recovery was slow. I could not walk more than ten steps without having to rest.

Mother had her own share of medical issues. She had to have a complete mastectomy and suffered a long and painful recovery.

At the beginning of 1945, conditions became more desperate and the Japanese more hateful. The human body needs salt in order to survive, especially in the tropics. The Japanese, in their infinite cruelty, decided to cut off our salt ration for a solid month, and the suffering began in earnest. People began to die of starvation, sometimes as many as three a day. The old, the sick, and those without religious faith were the first to die. Some, we believed, died because they had given up hope of ever being rescued. MacArthur had promised us that he would return, but he never said when. After the war, I discovered that he wanted the navy to bypass the Philippines, which would have meant death for all of us.

Toward the end of January 1945, we heard, via the bamboo telegraph, that the US Army had finally landed in the Philippines and that the Japs were retreating. Strange new aircraft flew over the camp wagging their wings "hello" at us. We were forbidden to turn the lights on at night. In the daytime, every time a US plane would fly over, the guards would hide underneath trees, leaving us to frantically wave. Near the end of our captivity, we started seeing light flashes from the plane's cannon and hearing the rumbles of the shots.

One night, we were awakened around midnight by guards ordering us to collect all the picks, shovels, and any other property that the Japs felt could be useful. We found out later that the soldiers had been sent to Manila to dig fortifications before the US Army could advance. Later that early morning, our captors simply vanished, and we found ourselves alone in camp.

We thought about leaving camp, but the Filipino guerillas in the area warned us to remain for our own safety. Soldiers had strict orders to shoot any escaping prisoners on sight. So instead, we broke into the Japanese food storage bins and gorged ourselves. Natives from the nearby town came into camp and brought us fresh fruit, coconuts, and vegetables. There had always been abundant food right outside the camp fences, but we were forbidden, under penalty of immediate execution, to harvest any of it. Someone found a Japanese radio, and we heard that eight hundred American ships had landed at Lingayan Gulf.

We feasted and had the camp to ourselves for one wonderful week until the Japanese, just as suddenly as they had vanished, rematerialized. At the realization that their war was lost, and on what we had done to the camp, they turned their anger and their frustration on us prisoners by reducing the food supply and passing new draconian regulations. Death became the immediate punishment for even a minor infraction of the rules. We began to be haunted by a terrifying fear that the Japs would wipe out the entire camp and then retreat if American troops ever reached Los Baños.

One morning, we were awakened by a rifle shot. Pat Hell, our camp gardener, along with a few of his friends, had been regularly escaping each night and going into the city of Los Baños to bring foodstuffs back to us. Pat was the first prisoner caught coming back under the wire, and he was shot in the shoulder for his trouble. The other internees who were with Pat hid outside the camp in coconut trees and could see every excruciating detail of what was to happen next. The guards left Pat out in the hot sun for hours before the order was given for his execution. An officer put his pistol to Pat's head and pulled the trigger. The other escaped internees returned that night. We did not have any more escapes.

After they had returned, the Japanese began severely cutting our rations. They had no use for prisoners, and providing for them was depleting their own diminishing rations. Even with our starvation rations, we were not dying fast enough to suit them. The Jap commandant declared, "We will have them eating mud before we are through."

By early February, the Japs issued us just enough unhusked rice to last three days if we only ate one meal a day. Luckily, there were some mestiza girls in the next unit who could unhusk the rice and winnow the chaff. They had a hollowed block of wood and pounded the rice with a baseball bat on that block to remove the husks from the rice kernels. They would then place the kernels on a large, round tray and flip it into the wind to discard the chaff. If it had not been for them, we would not have had anything at all to eat.

We were dying at the rate of three per day now. I was down to fifty-six pounds on my five-foot-four-inch frame. My knees knocked together so badly that I would almost trip myself. Pam was the only one of us who looked somewhat normal even though she was suffering just as much as the rest of us. In the hospital, Dad's beriberi was literally eating him alive, and the doctor told us he did not have long to live. We went to Mass every day and prayed.

On February 22, 1945, we finished digging a ditch around our barracks so we could catch rainwater runoff. We were pretty proud of our ingenuity. That evening, rumors began circulating that we were all going to be shot at morning roll call because we were still not dying fast enough. Every night we could see the flashes and hear the rumble of artillery, and those rumbles were getting closer by the day. The Japanese were obviously planning their retreat.

Pam's Recall

Our family volunteered to go to Los Baños, a new internment camp under construction at the site of the Philippine Agricultural College at Los Baños, near Laguna de Bay, a huge inland lake. (According to Hartendorp pages 247–48, we were bused to Los Baños April 7, 1944. We were about 531 persons: 192 were members of family units, 192 were unattached men, and 147 were unattached women. For an excellent account of what life was like for adults at Los Baños, including a description of the barracks, the physical and social organization of the camp, complete with drawings and photographs, see *Deliverance*, by Anthony.)

We were housed in barracks. Each barrack was constructed with a central dirt hall, bisected in the middle with another dirt hallway. Barracks held ninety-two people. On both sides of the hall were cubicles designed to hold two people. The walls of each cubicle did not reach the ceiling.

Because there were five in our family, we were assigned to two and one half cubicles. That meant that one cubicle was bisected, and the men moved the wall. My brothers had one cubicle; my parents, the middle cubicle; and I had the half cubicle. Doors were cut between our cubicles so we had access to the center room. All the outside doors were closed off so that there was only one front and one back door leading into and out of our parents' room.

The back door led outside to a covered dirt area, which we used as our sitting and dining room. This area was circumscribed by a large ditch we crossed by a wood plank. Then there was another dirt area we used for cooking in a lean-to. A path separated our cooking area from the bathing and toilet barracks.

On one side of us were the Laceys. Bill Lacey was ex-navy. He and his wife, Betty, had a three-year-old daughter, Sharon. I would take her for walks all over the camp. On our other side were the Hogenbooms, a Seventh-Day Adventist family who shared the canned meat from their Red Cross packages. They sang the Doxology before every meal holding hands.

Between each barracks used for living quarters was the barracks for toilets, showers, and sinks. Although the toilets were separated from the showers by a wall, toilets were simply a long row of open holes with a single collection area underneath. (The unique mechanism for flushing the toilets is described in *Deliverance*, 56–57.) It was easy to see which toilets were open and free. It was also easy to have conversations with the person sitting on the neighboring toilet. The showers were open gang showers. There was no hot water. One end of the barracks was the men's bathroom and the other end was for the women. A dirt hall ran through the middle of the barracks to allow access to the barracks on either side.

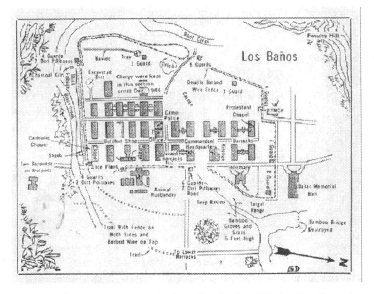

Map of Los Baños, including both the "Holy City" and
"Hell's Half Acre." By permission of Lou Gopal

Our barrack was close to the road that divided the two camps: the civilian camp and the "Holy City," or the part of the camp that later housed the missionaries. At one end of camp, one of the barracks was set aside for schoolrooms and a library. We children walked through all the barrack to go to school every day. At the other end of the camp, in the Holy City, was the chapel.

Arthur (79–92) describes the college-level courses that were given in Los Baños without benefit of textbooks or other teaching aids. Courses were taught from memory. He says the courses included Japanese, Spanish, Tagalog, economics, medieval and ancient world history, geology, paleontology, literature, philosophy, and freshman English. He made no mention of the equally well-qualified and dedicated teachers who taught in the grades and in high school. I remember struggling to learn sixth-grade fractions and having my father try to help me with my homework.

I borrowed many books from that library, but the one I loved the most was Frances Hodgson Burnett's *The Secret Garden*. One day a man brought his daughter, who was about my age, to the library. He would pick up books at random and scan them. He rejected *The Secret Garden* for his daughter. She seemed to be about my age, and I knew she would have loved the story. I was so angry at him for preventing his daughter from reading such a wonderful book.

I read a lot. The only problem with this form of distraction was that novels always have descriptions of people eating. So reading about food only made me hungrier.

Other than school, we children were free to roam the camp. One of the women tried to establish an afterschool activity for the girls by creating The Happy Hearts Club as a corollary to the Boy Rangers (based upon the Boy Scouts). I didn't think we were learning anything interesting like the Rangers, but it is probably where I learned to knit and to make tiny bears out of scraps of cloth stuffed with cotton.

The Boy Rangers were learning what I considered important things like semaphore code and tying knots. Although I could not be a Ranger, since I was a girl, my brothers were kind enough to teach me knots and semaphore code.

My brothers worked on small garden plots under Pat Held, the head gardener. Pat was later shot and killed returning to camp from a night trying to find and bring back food for the camp.

Since the cubicles were separated by partial walls not very high, we children would climb up and crawl all over the barracks looking in to see what people were doing. One day, one of the boys said he had seen two people "doing it" in their closet, so we all crawled along to see. When we found nothing at all, we were very disappointed.

When we originally arrived at Los Baños, it was a very large camp with lots of open space. Later, the fences were shifted so that we were given less space and freedom to move about.

All barracks opened onto a dirt street. Every morning when we turned out for roll call at 7:00 a.m., we left the barracks, crossed the ditch, and lined up in two rows. On the other side of the road was the fenced living area for the soldiers.

One day, one of the guards organized an expedition for the children. He took us on a walk outside the camp through immense beautiful trees. When Mother heard about it, she scolded me and told me never to do that again. She was frantic, as she had no idea where I was.

Joan Silen and I were "best friends" even though she lived in a different barracks with her two older sisters and her mother. One of the games we used to play was to try to leap from a bench to a low tree limb that was just outside the hospital building. We couldn't understand why we had to move the bench closer and closer to the tree. All the books we had read said that exercise made a person grow stronger and develop muscles. That we were getting less and less food to eat, which made us weaker, never entered our heads.

Mother was assigned to work in the kitchens. Here she met the prostitutes who had come to Los Baños with us. I think it was the first time she had ever met a prostitute, and found them delightful companions, full of laughter and fun and not afraid to work.

As food became even scarcer, mother sold her circle of diamonds for a promised ten kilos of rice. She received five. By that time, our daily ration of food was a butter tin of unhusked rice, which had to be pounded and husked before it was edible. (Tins of butter were about the size of a small tin of canned tuna fish today.) I remember wandering around the camp looking for food. Sometimes there was leftover food in the guards' garbage cans. Sometimes I would break off the heads of hibiscus flowers to eat.

Joan and I decided to try another way to get some food. We went to the guardhouse at the fence line near the chapel and just stood staring at the soldiers. They became quite agitated and tried to get us to leave, indicating they would get in trouble if their officer found us there. We stubbornly refused to move till they gave us some food and sugar in a banana leaf. We ate some of the food, divided what was left, and took the rest home to our families.

One day, Mother went to the hospital for a bilateral radical mastectomy. Since there was no diagnostic equipment, Dr. Nance had no idea whether her breast lumps were benign or malignant. He did the surgery as a preventive measure. Mother had to leave the hospital, however, when Dad collapsed and was hospitalized. I remember her washing towels and hanging them on the line so she could maintain upper body flexibility. I would watch her cry as she would lift heavy wet towels and pin them to the clothesline. Every day the clothesline was set a little higher so she had to reach higher. She was in excruciating pain as well when she removed the bandages from her open wounds to change her own dressings.

Dad spent the rest of our internment bedridden in the hospital with severe beriberi (both legs were so swollen he could not walk) where the navy nurses and some of the Catholic nuns provided the nursing care. One day when Mother was visiting, she confided to one of the nuns that she was angry because Dad was dying. The nun told her, "Why don't you tell God all about it?" So Mother went to the chapel and told God off. Then she went back to the hospital and told Dad off. She accused him of taking the easy way out and dying, leaving her alone with the responsibility of three children. I will never know whether Dad was too shocked to die, but he was still alive when we were rescued on February 23, 1945.

One day the fence was taken down between the "Holy City" and us. The Protestant and Catholic missionaries were housed in the "Holy City." One barracks held all the Catholic nuns. (I was never able to understand how these women managed to keep their white habits clean with only cold water for washing and how they managed to starch and iron their wimples!) Having decided I was going to grow up and be a nun, I made friends with a Good Shepherd sister and a Maryknoll nun—Sister Patricia Marie. Sister Patricia Marie taught us our catechism in preparation for the Sacrament of Confirmation, which was held in November 1944. There were a number of orders of missionary priests as well. I never knew any of the Protestant missionary families.

One day, when we went outside for morning roll call, there were no guards. The men searched the camp, but there were no soldiers anywhere and no signs of where they had gone. Someone dug out a flag, another took out of hiding a contraband radio and played the news for the entire camp. The first song we heard was Roy Rogers singing "Don't Fence Me In." Then one day the soldiers returned just as unexpectedly as they had left, and life became even harder and food even scarcer.

The only thing we thought about was food and being rescued. People who had been sharing their meager rations of food with their dog found that someone had killed and eaten it. The men, who generally just wore a pair of shorts, looked like walking skeletons. The women, in their weathered wash dresses, looked thin but not starved. (Men lose weight faster than women, as any woman who has gone to Weight Watchers with her husband can tell you.) As Sister Patricia Marie told me years later, I never looked as if I had been starving.

Although our lives were bad in Los Baños, it was far better than what the internees suffered at Santo Thomas. I remain grateful to my father for making the decision to transfer us to Los Baños for the remainder of our war.

Chapter 9

WE ARE RESCUED BY THE GRACE OF GOD

Bill's Story

February 23 came. So did the Airborne, the amtracs, and the guerillas. They met at 7:00 a.m. at Los Baños Internment Camp. I was starting a fire in our clay stove and had a ringside view of the C-47s coming in. The little white clouds turned out to be paratroopers.

"Duck; get in the trenches; keep your heads down!" Firing was in progress all around us, then a lull. Some very fat American soldiers came by.

"Take what you can carry and get down to the field." We did. On the way, we passed beheaded Japs in a ditch.

We reached the field as amtracs were coming through the bamboo fence. They towered above us.

"Your father has already gone with the hospital patients. Get on this one." We mounted on one with the ramp down.

On the way down to Lake Laguna de Bay, we heard pings on the metal of the amtrac. Snipers. We drove right into the lake and away from the shore. Part of our number were left on the beach for a second trip. They had been able to walk to the shore.

During our trip, we were under machine-gun fire. We could watch the splashes go by the tanks. One of the young men, Nelson, sat on the top of one and was shot through the leg. He survived. He drew a hole in his cast where the bullet had penetrated.

Bob's Story

On February 23, we rose at dawn for our normal roll call at 7:00 a.m. Bill and I planned to work the day in the camp gardens. Bill had just lit the breakfast fire when an airplane flying over camp started disgorging something that looked like people diving toward the camp. Once the parachutes blossomed from their backs, our hopes soared. Two more planes flew over the camp, and paratroopers began falling to earth. Because it was early in the morning, as per their ritual, our Japanese guards had stripped to their loincloths and were exercising. Their rifles were neatly stacked out of easy reach. They were caught completely by surprise.

Somebody shouted, "Those are Americans. Jump in the ditch." We quickly dove into our newly dug ditch as guns began firing all around us. I was sorely tempted to raise my head to see what was going on, but I restrained myself. The bullets went through our barracks' walls as if they were made of paper. Some *nipa* walls caught fire due to tracer rounds.

Suddenly it was very quiet. I slowly raised my head. No one shot at us, and we climbed out of the ditch. A large American soldier walked up to us. He looked well fed, and he was twice the size of the Japanese soldiers we were used to.

All he had to say was, "Any Japs around here?" and utter pandemonium broke out. Women ran up to him and kissed him, and the men pounded him on the back. At that moment, all we wanted to do was exult that we were free, and our Japanese captors were either killed or running for their lives.

We were told, over and over again, to gather our belongings and assemble on the road in front of the barracks. All that I owned, a shirt and a pair of pants, fit into my pillowcase. All of our friends and neighbors were gathering there. We were told to proceed toward the church and the gym and the front gate, and freedom. The barracks started to burn. I learned later that the army deliberately set fire to the barracks to get us to move. As we approached the front gate, a dead Jap soldier was lying in a ditch. We were told not to look. Everybody looked at the body.

We walked down toward Laguna de Bay, where amtracs, heavily armored and amphibious vehicles, awaited us on shore. We saw my father for the first time in weeks, He had gotten so weak that he could not walk. Dad and other hospital patients were loaded onto one of the first amtracs because of their conditions. Mother, Bill, Pam, and I were loaded on another. Once loaded, the amtracs started their journey across the bay.

Pam's Story

On February 23, 1945, American and guerrilla forces liberated Los Baños Internment Camp. Not a single civilian died in the raid.

TIME Magazine. Monday, Apr 16, 1945. Letters to the Editor:

Wonderful Rescue

Sirs: My brother-in-law, Myron E. Brink, sent this letter written in lead pencil to be typed and sent to you. Mr. Brink was President of the Cebu Chamber of Commerce ... "After being starved, robbed, and kicked around for three years, we were rescued yesterday from the Los Baños Internment Camp. Yesterday we were to have eaten banana stalks. That was all and the Japs said there would be no more food. About sunrise our planes came over, dropped paratroops and engaged our guards. The guerrillas also attacked, and during the fighting our tanks drove in through our prison walls. We were hurried into these tanks and started out. It was a wonderful sight to see this string of 70 tanks in perfect formation traveling steadily toward freedom through the water. Imagine 150 American boys rescuing and transporting over 2,000 prisoners out of a territory surrounded by 6,000 Japs. We left behind us many graves filled with starved internees ... Our Army men and officers certainly are angels … Oh! how wonderful it is to be an American!" … MABEL F. RICE Whittier, Calif."

The day began like any other day. We were getting ready for roll call at 7:00 a.m. My brother Bill was at the little stove in our lean-to trying to start a fire for our morning coffee (or whatever it was that we were using for coffee). When we heard the planes, we all went outdoors to look. We had been seeing planes flying over and knew that the Americans were back in the Philippines. It was always a wonderful sight to see those huge planes flying over in formation. But today was different. As we watched, we saw what looked like puffs of smoke from the planes. What was going on?

Soon there was an excited buzz that swept through the camp. Paratroopers! Paratroopers were landing! We were being rescued! People began to dance around and yell wildly.

Mother screamed at Bill to stop working on the coffee and get a mat from the house and put it in the ditch. Then she made us crawl into the ditch. By this time, we could hear gunfire, screaming and yelling, and general chaos. We wanted to peek out of the ditch to see what was going on, but Mother screamed at us to keep our heads down. It was frightening not knowing what was happening but knowing it wasn't good.

When we could no longer hear the gunfire, we looked up and saw an American soldier with a very dirty face walking by carrying a gun. He grinned at us and asked, "Where are the Japs?"

Word came that we were to leave immediately. "Take what you can, and get out! Walk down the street toward the front of the camp." I could not carry my Betsey Wetsey or Patsy Ann, my rag doll, and had to leave them behind. What I brought out with me was the small prayer book Father Gries gave me as a baptismal present and a belt made from painted coconut shells I had received as a gift for my tenth birthday. (I still have them both.)

Mother gathered us together, and we set off down the road with all the other internees. People would stop and look in the ditch, point and laugh. I wanted to look too when I was told they were looking at a dead Japanese soldier. Mother wouldn't let me.

When we got to the end of the camp, we all milled around waiting to be put on trucks. We could smell smoke. The barracks had been set on fire.

There are a number of books and documentaries of our rescue. It was remarkable that no prisoner was killed during the fighting.

Not long after the war, we received a small pamphlet written by Father William McCarthy called *The Angels Came at Seven*. Mother was so hurt that of all the people Father McCarthy talked about in his story, we were not mentioned at all.

The trucks unloaded us when we got to the amtracs, which took us across the lake (Laguna de Bay). We were told to keep our heads down while we were crossing the lake in the amtracs. Evidently one man had not done so and was shot by a sniper, but only wounded.

Chapter 10

New Bilibid and Being Sent Home on a Hospital Ship

Bill's Memories

We were taken to New Bilibid prison to be fed soup for a week, then solid food, before we were well enough to be sent home to the United States I gained 1½ pounds a day for thirty days, going from ninety-seven pounds to 143 pounds. Most of the weight seemed to come in lumps. We were taken to the US *Torrens* on landing craft. We left with a nice convoy bound for San Francisco. Not long after we left the islands, we turned south in the company of three destroyer escorts. We were headed for the New Hebrides to pick up five hundred wounded sailors.

I was playing cards with a young soldier around midnight after our southern turn. There was a sharp metallic clanging that seemed to travel the length of the ship.

We had been torpedoed. The tin fish had slid the length of the *Torrens*. Next morning the three DEs were gone. From then on, we sailed alone.

One day we pulled into a tropical harbor. A sight we saw was the sunken hulk of some of our interisland steamers. One was the *Luzon*.

We moored and loaded the sailors. Even with them on board, there were empty holds on the ship. From that harbor, we zigzagged our way east to San Francisco alone.

I don't think there was a dry eye in our numbers as we went under the Golden Gate Bridge to begin our final land trip home.

Bob's Memories

At New Bilibid, we were given breakfast cereal, and nothing has ever tasted so good. I tasted real sugar for the first time in over a year, and I could not get enough. While we were on the water, Japs started shooting at us from the safety of the hills. The bullet impacts were like watching rain on the water. Our gunner opened up with a .50-caliber machine gun and hot casings spilled into the bay and into the amtrac. Bill kept one of the casings. One internee was wounded because he foolishly mooned himself on the cab of the amtrac.

We found out later that our rescue consisted of a three-pronged attack. A motorized column came up toward the Japanese line and diverted their attention to it. An amphibious force crossed Laguna de Bay, after they had liberated New Bilibid Prison, and evacuated the liberated internees. The third force had the most dangerous mission: using nine C-46s, paratroopers were dropped on the camp precisely at the guards' exercise time to free the internees. It worked like clockwork. The Los Baños raid is among the most perfectly executed military operations in history. The only reason it did not land on the front page of every newspaper in America was that a soon-to-be-famous photograph graced those pages instead: the marines landing on Iwo Jima.

We landed on the opposite shore, where New Bilibid Prison was located. The army had freed the camp the day before. We were assigned cells, since it was a prison. The doors stayed open at all times. Our cots were double bunks with wooden slats instead of mattresses. We were given pillows and blankets, and most of our fellow former internees chose to sleep on the ground outside because we were so skinny that it hurt too much to sleep on bare wood. Just like back at the club, we were separated by gender and age. Dad was in the prison hospital; Mother and Pam were with the other women and girls. We were able to get together each day.

Our first meal was soup. The army had learned, from bitter

experience with the internees from Santo Tomas, that if we were given regular food, we might die. We overate anyway. We got in line, ate our soup, and then got back in line for seconds and thirds. They finally had to cut us off. I remember lying in my bunk that first night with a bloated stomach thinking that I could have more. Sadly, one of my teenage buddies ate a whole combat ration bar and died. (See the letter from Maude Brink to her mother and sister about our rescue in the appendix, dated February 24, 1945.)

The Japanese made one futile attempt to capture our new camp. They made a *banzai* attack but were quickly mowed down. We settled into a daily routine that consisted of mostly eating and getting to know some of the soldiers. Dad was improving and was even able to walk around some.

We were issued army khakis and combat boots, which I was surprised to learn had to be eleven and one-half inches long to fit. After going barefoot or wearing *bakyas* for the last three years, my feet had not only grown, but my toes were splayed out and had to get used to being inside footwear again.

Every afternoon, some soldiers would pass out candy bars, chewing gum, and cigarettes to each person. We kids didn't smoke, so the cigarettes were given to our parents. I was about five feet four inches and weighed fifty-six pounds. At the beginning of the war, I was two inches shorter and had weighed 101 pounds. Neither Bill, who was five inches taller than me, nor Mother weighed one hundred pounds. All of us internees were in the same boat. We looked like walking skeletons. Thankfully, we all started gaining weight, and our health improved dramatically. Soon it would be time for the long ocean voyage to America, our new home. I had always lived in the Philippines. Our next stop was Auntie Mable and Grandmother's house in Whittier, California.

Finally, the army felt that we were in good enough condition to travel (even internees like Dad). (See the letter written from New Bilibid prison by Myron Brink to his brother Millard in March 1945, in the appendix.)

We were loaded into trucks and driven to Manila. It was a lot happier trip this time, as there were no Japanese soldiers around, and we had plenty to eat and drink. Manila City had been called the "Pearl of the Orient" before the war, but when we arrived, we could tell that the Japanese had not given up without a fight. Our soldiers sometimes had to fight from room to room, and, in many cases, we could see the multiple bullet holes in the walls. We were taken out to the harbor and loaded onto a Liberty ship. Liberty ships were small ships usually hulled with concrete and were used primarily to transport troops or carry cargo. We became a vast armada of ships that stretched as far as the eye could see. Our armada headed toward Leyte, and there we parted company from the convoy and sailed off in the company of three destroyer escorts.

The Liberty ship was nothing like any of the ocean liners I had known. First, they were not luxury ships. They were troop carriers. The hold, where we slept, was tiered eight high with bunk beds that could be folded into the wall. There was barely enough room to turn over. We had to bathe in salt water, and we could not generate any foam from the soap. I felt sticky and never felt clean. We shared the hold with returning army troops. The food was good, and we were free to go up on deck. The women were sequestered in a restricted section of the ship. Mother and several of her cronies made cream puffs for everyone on board one day, for which the crew and the GIs were grateful. Bill and I put on a boxing exhibition for the troops that was well-received.

Our little convoy eventually arrived at Espirito Santo, the capitol of the New Hebrides Islands. It was a tranquil spot, and the troops went swimming. They dived or jumped over the side of the ship and really enjoyed themselves. Our ship's mission was to pick up several hundred seamen who had been on the island for over a year and transport them home as well. Even though the ship was crammed full with the army and the navy and us internees, we all got along because we were going home!

The ocean is a wondrous place. We sailed across stretches of it where the water would be so translucent we could see miles into its depths. I spotted water sprites far off in the distance. Sometimes porpoises would accompany us, and schools of them would leap in front of the bow. We even saw a pod of whales. I got my sea legs by the second day. I pity the people who were attacked with seasickness.

Several days out of Espirito Santo, we encountered a typhoon. Since our ship had little ballast, we were tossed like a cork on the water, and I loved it. The soldiers we had sailed with from Manila had their sea legs and were not bothered at all by the tossing about of the storm. The poor sailors had not gotten acclimated yet and took a lot of ribbing from the army guys because they were all seasick and heaving over the side.

One night, a few days after the storm, I was awakened by the sound of something thumping the hull. This happened three times. We had all performed lifeboat drills, and I grabbed my life preserver, jumped out of my bunk, and hurried on deck. Once I got topside, an alarm went off, and I could see one subchaser streaming smoke with fire coming out of its funnel as it sped away on the hunt. We found out later that a Jap submarine had attacked us, and the hull noises I heard were the sound of torpedoes scrapping the bottom of our ship. The torpedoes were set to destroy a large water-heavy target. Since we had no ballast, the torpedoes never encountered anything to set their charges. We never saw the other subchasers again.

Our remaining trip to our ultimate destination, San Francisco, was calm. Somewhere along the way, we got word that Franklin Roosevelt had died, and Harry Truman was the new president. Dad never cared for FDR.

As we entered San Francisco Bay, tracer rounds were shot in a long arc overhead to welcome us home. When we eventually docked, a band greeted us. Whether it was for us or the soldiers or the sailors, no one cared. We had arrived.

Pam's Memories

On the other side of the lake, we were unloaded from the amtracs and reloaded onto another string of trucks to take us to New Bilibid. In *Deliverance,* there is a photograph of two men waiting to be loaded onto a truck. The picture is labeled, "two old men," and one, sitting on the ground with his legs stretched out in front of him, was my father. The patients from the hospital had been loaded first and were the first to arrive at New Bilibid, a prison set aside for us. As we drove into the prison, we could see a line of internees in a food line. Dad was standing up in line with them!

For the first three days after our rescue, we were fed only soup. (Evidently when some of the internees at Santo Thomas were confronted with real food, they ate too much and died.) We spent every day just standing in line for food. As soon as we finished one bowl, we would get back in line for the next.

Our rescue was filmed, and parts of it are available on YouTube. We were told that these films were shown in theaters at home for friends and relatives, to see if they could identify family members. The first reel includes the internees being loaded on trucks, crossing Laguna de Bay in amtracs, the Red Cross ambulance trucks arriving at New Bilibid, standing in line for food, and a flight over the camp. Reel 2 contains aerial shots of the camp and amtracs crossing the bay. Reel 3 has clips of internees getting off trucks after arriving in New Bilibid, and people signing in and receiving Red Cross supplies. The reel includes a very pretty young woman wearing shorts. The photographer evidently liked her legs! There are shots of children with chocolate, and some nuns. Reel 4 once again shows us standing in line for soup and washing our own dishes, with another segment of unloading a truck on arrival.

We were housed in open rooms containing iron double beds. Mother and I were in a different cellblock from my brothers, and Dad had been taken to a hospital building, where he stayed the entire time we were in New Bilibid. We were given supplies, and the Red Cross gave us women's army boots to wear. We had gone barefooted for so long our feet were quite wide and hard to fit. I was fitted with size 7 women's army boots.

I do not remember having school of any kind at New Bilibid. My friends and I were free to roam the prison so long as we did not get too close to the walls. One day we found the building with the electric chair. Fortunately, the electricity was turned off. The GIs were very kind to us. They shared their chocolate rations with us just as they shared their cigarettes with the adults. Some would take us out of the camp in a truck to go swimming, under guard, at a nearby swimming pool. One soldier befriended me, and we corresponded for months after I had returned to the States.

My father had been a curly redhead. When we were rescued, his hair was completely white. By the time we were ready to leave New Bilibid, my father's hair was red again. The doctors told Mother that if they knew what caused his hair to return to its normal color, they could make a fortune.

We stayed in New Bilibid until we were strong enough to leave for home.

Finally, the day came when trucks arrived, and we were driven to Manila to the port, where we were to board ship with other internees from other camps. We were assigned to a hospital ship, a converted troop ship, because Dad was not fully recovered. Joan Silen and her family were with us as one of Joan's sisters had been shot in the hip during our rescue from *Los Baños*.

We children roamed the ship at will. The sailors were very kind and patient with us. I remember being allowed on the bridge and being allowed to steer the ship. I was given a compass point to watch closely so I did not deviate off-course. I hope the sailor who gave us this exceptional experience was not punished too badly for his kindness. Many of us slept on deck at night because the holds where we were housed were so hot. I had the fun of babysitting a two-year old. We would wander the ship together holding hands. One day, we looked through a hole in the side of the ship and watched as the water streamed by. Her mother found us and told me never to do that again, as the baby might fall through the hole. I had never thought of that.

My mother and a friend of hers decided to do something special for the sailors who were taking us home. Although we were thrilled with the food we were given, the sailors were bored with the never-changing menu. Mother went to the head cook and asked him if he had the ingredients for cream puffs. He said he thought he did. They converted her memorized recipe serving six to eight people into cream puffs for the entire ship! The ship's kitchen staff was delighted to participate in the "surprise." The cream puffs were a great success.

We began our journey across the Pacific in a convoy of ships until one day when we turned away from the convoy and sailed south alone. We headed for New Guinea to pick up Seabees. (My brothers say we went to the New Hebrides.)

The trip home was essentially uneventful except for the night we were torpedoed. The torpedo missed, just scraping the hull, but the ship was shaken badly. During our trip, we were all examined for lice, including pubic lice, by the navy nurses. I had never heard of pubic lice.

Then one day, as we approached land, we saw an enormous beautiful bridge. Excitement raced through the ship when we learned it was the Golden Gate Bridge. We had arrived in San Francisco!

Chapter 11

BECOMING AMERICANS

Bob's Story

After we offloaded from the ship, we stayed at a hotel downtown. It had this wondrous thing called an elevator that I could operate myself. I don't know how many trips I took on that thing. Dad and Mother took us shopping for clothes. They had no idea how to dress us, and I wound up in a three-piece brown suit. While we were out shopping, a car backfired, and we all hit the dirt. People looked at us as if we were crazy.

We took the Super Chief train to Los Angeles and were met there by Auntie Mabel. She drove us to her home in Whittier, and I met my grandmother Rice for the first time that I could remember.

Pam's Story

It was May 1945. My family arrived in San Francisco via troop ship. We were among the thousands of internees who had been rescued from Japanese internment camps in the Philippines. By the time our ship arrived, the debarkation procedures at the port of San Francisco were well established. Our family went to a hotel. My only vivid memory of our stay in San Francisco was a trip to a department store with Mother to buy clothes. When I got bored, I left Mother's side and wandered around the store. I met a kindly woman, and we got into a conversation. I went outside with her onto the sidewalk, where Mother found me. Mother was frantic with worry. Just as she was scolding me, a car drove by and backfired. Mother and I hit the sidewalk. We were very embarrassed when we saw no one else had even noticed the noise. It took us a long time to stop ducking every time we heard a loud noise. We learned later that we were shell-shocked.

I have no recall of the train trip; I have a vague sense of getting off the train and the long walk with many other people to the waiting area.

We were met at the train station in Los Angeles by my mother's sister, Mabel Rice. We spent the next month at Auntie Mabel's house in Whittier, California. At that time, Whittier was a small college town with a population of fifteen thousand surrounded by groves of avocado and orange trees.

Auntie Mabel taught at Whittier College, and her house was less than a block from the college campus. Auntie Mabel was famous for her course on children's literature and was a fixture in the Department of Education. She supported us financially and emotionally for years. Not only did we have no money, and Dad had no job, we were in debt for all the loans Dad had taken out while we were in prison camp. He tried to get compensation for our losses through the War Claims Office in Washington DC, but never seemed to fill out the forms the way some clerk wanted. Copies of his letters show his frustrations. We were never compensated by the War Claims Office as we had been promised. (See my father's letter to his brother documenting our poverty.)

Auntie Mabel gave up her bedroom to my parents, and she slept in her den on the first floor of the house. My brothers were given the bedroom usually rented out to a college student, and I was given an open porch type room. In each room, grandmother and Auntie Mabel had left us gifts. In addition, their friends and neighbors had donated hand-me-down clothes so we had something to wear.

About a month after our arrival, we moved to a rental house not far from Auntie Mabel's house. Also, at about this time, Dad got my brother Bill a job as a busboy at the Whittier College cafeteria. From his earnings, Bill bought himself a Dodge coup roadster with a rumble seat.

We were not far from downtown Whittier, and I remember walking to town every day to go shopping for silly little girl things, looking in store windows and going to movies at the Roxy or the Wardman theaters. (The Roxy no longer exists, and the Wardman is the only movie theater left in town.) Dad gave us an allowance of four dollars (I don't remember if it was by week or month.) I spent a goodly amount of it on five-cent candy bars. What a treat for a little girl who had been starving just months before. I gained weight rapidly that year.

I have a vivid memory of proudly announcing to the ticket seller at the Roxy theater in September that I was now twelve years old and would no longer be paying the children's price of twelve cents. I was now an adult and would be paying thirty-five cents for the movies. In those days, going to the movies meant two feature films, short shorts, Movietone News, and cartoons.

Late that summer, I met a boy my age who befriended me. We spent hours riding our bikes around town and telling each other all about ourselves, our hopes and dreams. He was very kind. One day, he invited me to go to the movies with him, and I agreed. I was surprised when both he and his parents showed up at Auntie Mabel's house. My parents decided it was all right for me to go to the movies with these strangers. Not long after, he moved away from Whittier, and I never saw him again.

Eventually my parents found a house they both liked. It was of stucco with a red Spanish tile roof. Situated on a hillside, the front entrance was at one level and the back door led down fifteen steps to the two-car garage, the three avocado trees, and two orange trees in the back yard. It was a three-bedroom house with the bedrooms on the left connected by a corridor or hallway that separated the bedrooms from the rest of the house. Between the master bedroom and the next bedroom was the master bath with a tub/shower. At the end of the hallway was a small toilet with sink. The small back hallway had a large washtub next to the back door. The front entrance of the house opened into the large living room with a picture window. An arched door led into the dining room. Another door led to the breakfast room on the right, and still another door led from the dining room to the kitchen. It was a house of many doors.

Initially we had an icebox. The iceman would climb up the back stairs to the kitchen and place the huge cube of ice in the icebox. The back door was always left open for him. The milkman delivered bottles of milk to the front door, and the first person home was responsible for putting the milk away in the icebox.

Dad bought a 1938 Buick sedan that had a floor stick shift. When Mother bought a new Pontiac sedan in 1949, that car was passed down to Bob and then eventually to me. Bill always had a job and bought his own cars. I was a senior in high school when I got the car.

The day the war was formally declared over in August, Dad and I were out shopping. We joined everyone else with yelling and shouting and blaring our car horn.

In September when school was about to start, Dad took me to the Bailey Junior High School to enroll me in the seventh grade and meet my teachers. I believe he did the same thing with my brothers at Whittier Union High School.

I walked to school or rode my bike. In the winter, mornings in Southern California are cool, but afternoons are warm. I walked or rode downhill in the mornings but trudged uphill in the afternoons. We were over a mile from school. If I wanted to go downtown, I walked or took my bike. Nestled in the hills above our house was a riding stable where I spent many Saturdays grooming horses and mucking out stables to earn a riding lesson.

My brothers and I were misfits at school. We talked differently. We pronounced many words with a British accent. We did not speak slang. We were objects of great curiosity, and everyone wanted to hear about the atrocities we had seen. That seems to have been all anyone wanted to hear about. When I could share no horror stories, people lost interest in me. I was very lonely.

I still get irritated when people try to compare our experiences as prisoners under the Japanese in the Pacific with the German prison camps. Other than the brutality of the guards and systematic starvation, these camps had little in common. The Germans were trying to exterminate their own citizens following the principles of eugenics. The Japanese were dealing with prisoners of war—both soldiers and civilians—of foreign nations with different customs and traditions. Male prisoners were beaten, shot, and beheaded; the women were raped. It was only at the very end that the Japanese decided to kill us all. (After we were rescued, we were told that on the morning of our rescue, the machine guns were trained on where we would have been standing at roll call. We were all to have been killed that morning.) Trying to compare the two experiences is to belittle the sufferings of civilian POWs under the Japanese. It is one of the reasons so few of us have told our stories.

My best friend that first year of school was a girl from a missionary family who had lived in Africa. We had a lot in common growing up outside of the United States. Neither of us had grown up in Whittier and had no school friends from elementary school. It was good to have a friend. She was no longer there in the eighth grade.

I was still wearing the WAC boots I had been given at New Bilibid, but the principal told Mother I needed to wear shoes. The other children were making fun of me. We had a lot of trouble finding shoes that fit, as my feet were so broad. The shoe store had an X-ray machine where I could stand on the base and look down at my feet in the shoes to see if they fit correctly. I really didn't want to give up those boots. I have no recall of what kind of shoes Mother bought, but Spectator shoes were in fashion so I may have had them.

My mother was an excellent cook and seamstress. Dad bought her a Singer sewing machine with a foot pedal. She made most of my clothes for years and often made clothing items as Christmas gifts. Initially, she insisted that we eat meals at the dining room table. I was responsible for setting the table, then cleaning up after meals. We children were responsible for doing the dishes and were supposed to rotate the duty, but my brother Bob often took a book and retired to the bathroom right after dinner. Bill didn't mind washing dishes as much as I did, so I dried and put away. This was the year I learned to make beds, clean bathrooms, vacuum rugs, dust mop the hardwood floors, and iron. Mother had a wringer washing machine, and I learned to hang the clothes out to dry on the clotheslines on the back deck over the garage. My brothers were responsible for yard maintenance.

I was given a remarkable amount of freedom to explore Whittier and go wherever I wanted to go without supervision of any kind. I spent a great deal of time alone. Other than the movie theaters on the weekends, the library was a favorite destination downtown with a wonderful selection of children's books. We rarely listened to the radio except for the news. Later, when we abandoned formal dining, we would sit together in the breakfast room listening to the programs on radio while we ate dinner. There was, of course, no television.

Not long after we arrived in Whittier, we began to renew contact with old friends from Cebu. Many had settled in Southern California.

Dad finally wore out. Sometime between my birthday on September 24 and when he died in October, he became bedridden, wracked with violent unremitting hiccoughs that could be heard all over the house. He was hospitalized finally and died in October 1945, in acute kidney failure, among other medical issues. The funeral home director told Mother later that the funeral cortege for my father's burial at Rose Hills Cemetery was the longest he had ever seen. Both Mother and Dad had given talks about the internment camp experience. Coupled with Auntie Mabel's reputation, we were well-known as the only POWs in town.

After Dad died, Mother had to cope with bills, no income, no job, and three children. We would not have survived without Auntie Mabel's help.

During the summer of 1946, Mother's cousin, Helen Knope, came for a visit with her family. Most memorable about that visit was the trip to Knott's Berry Farm. Here we are. I am on the left; Bob is on the right with Mother just behind him. Bill is in the back. The others are our cousins, the Knopes.

Trip to Knott's Berry Farm

In the fall of 1946, Mother began teaching eighth grade at the Bailey School on an emergency teaching credential. From that time on, her life consisted of teaching and going to school to earn her bachelor's degree and eventually her master's degree. She went to school Saturdays and summer vacations, getting up early in the morning to study before we all left for school, in addition to full-time teaching.

That first year after we arrived in the States is mostly a blur. These few snapshot memories are all I have of those days. It was a time of learning how to fit into a whole new world and way of doing things. It was a time of massive losses and upheavals and equally massive adjustments, a time to learn how to be an American.

A lasting legacy of those years has been my attitude toward food. I am never satisfied, even if full. Always hungry. Always looking for something to eat. Bill told me that he had never been able to share food, whether offering to let someone have a taste of his food or at home when he had company and prepared meals for them. It was always a wrench. Always a difficult effort to share.

There is a mistaken impression that children forget easily. Not so. Children suppress bad memories and eventually embody them. The memories are expressed in behaviors, illnesses, or an inability to handle intimacy. My brothers and I were fortunate in having loving parents who tried to protect us in every way they could in the midst of their own fears and anxieties. No matter what, they always made us feel safe and wanted. And that is the best legacy of all.

Chapter 12

THE REST OF THE STORY

Mother began teaching the eighth grade at the Bailey Junior High School on an emergency credential in the fall of 1946. That year I was also in the eighth grade at Bailey and my brothers were at Whittier Union High School. Mother drove the 1938 Buick to work, I rode my bike or walked, and my brothers drove together to school in one of Bill's series of cars. Mother never talked about money or how she was handling the debts incurred by the war.

My father had taken out life insurance policies for each of us children, which were to be used for our college educations. They matured on our eighteenth birthdays. Mother later told me that when the boys' policies matured, she used their money to pay for groceries. When my policy matured in 1951, I was able to use it to pay the tuition and fees for college.

In 1949, mother took us on a cross-country trip to Stephen's Point, Wisconsin, to try to locate her normal school records. She bought a new Pontiac for the trip. We took advantage of the trip to visit Bryce, Zion, the Grand Canyon, the Painted Desert, Mount Rushmore, and Yellowstone national parks and to visit old friends. In Albuquerque, we saw the Millings (the people whose house we moved into when they left for the States). Evangeline Hawk and her mother also lived there, but Evan refused to see me. Her mother said it was because I reminded her of her father. I was crushed. At Stephen's Point we stayed with Mother's cousin, Helen Johnson Knope, and her family. We went to Mackinaw Island, where Mother had spent a summer as a hotel maid. It was a memorable trip. Mother was able to find her school records, essential for her credits toward her bachelor's degree.

Riding in the surrey with Mother's cousin
Grace on Mackinaw Island 1949

Bill, Bob, Pam at the Grand Canyon 1949

Mother taught the eighth grade until her mandatory retirement in 1962. She never recovered from being made to retire one year before she had expected to retire. The principal explained it was to save the district money. She felt personally betrayed by her principal, and became very depressed. One day, in her eighties, she decided she had had a heart attack and went to bed and never got up again. Bill hired a home health aide to take care of her when he was at school. Eventually, he found her care too much of a burden and asked me to take care of her. I put Mother in a nursing home; and when I moved to Iowa, I took her with me.

One nice thing I was able to do for Mother was to give her a hot-air balloon ride for her ninetieth birthday. Mother loved to fly. The company brought the balloon and all the equipment to take off from the grounds of the nursing home so the staff and patients could enjoy the spectacle. Unfortunately, when I moved to Canada, Canada refused to allow me to bring her with me. She died alone in the nursing home in Iowa City in 1989.

When Bill graduated from Whittier High, he decided to study business at Fullerton Junior College. (Junior colleges in California were tuition free.) When he found he had no interest in business, he decided to join the air force and become a pilot. Unfortunately, Bill was colorblind, and so washed out of that program. He remained as an enlisted man and was trained in the radio service. Mother and I were home one Saturday when an FBI agent came to interview us about Bill. Bill volunteered to go to Japan to be as close as possible to his high school friends who were serving in the army in Korea. His last year in the service was spent at Andrews AFB outside of Washington, DC. On his way home after discharge, he went to Parkston, South Dakota, to meet the Brink family. He came home with some of the pots and pans our father had sold as a traveling salesman to pay his way through college.

When Bill came home from the air force, he enrolled at Whittier College to study geology under the GI Bill. He completed both his bachelor's and master's degrees at Whittier before moving to Blythe, California, where he taught at both the elementary school and the junior college. He was a volunteer with the Sheriff's Department, where his assignment was to fly over the area searching for downed airplanes. He was also a volunteer with the Coast Guard, patrolling the river on the weekends in his boat.

He left Blythe and moved back to Whittier to teach at the East Whittier school system after an incident at Blyth. He had been searching for a downed plane, looking for survivors. Instead, he found dead bodies scattered around that had been ravaged by predators. He gave up flying motorized airplanes and learned to soar.

At East Whittier, Bill served as a vice principal as well as a lower-grades teacher. For a few years, he had the best job in the world. East Whittier instituted what they called an "Outdoor School." The sixth-grade children were sent to the mountains for one week, where Bill taught them botany, biology, geology, and astronomy. He loved it and so did the children. Every summer for two weeks, Bill went to Wickenburg, Arizona, for tennis camp as well as to every Elderhostel he thought interesting.

When Bill took early retirement, he started square dancing classes and took a job at Knott's Berry Farm as the park ranger. During these years in Whittier, Bill continued boating and kept his boat at Santa Monica. He invited me along a couple of times for some deep-sea fishing and bought me my own fishing tackle. When he left Whittier, he gave his boat to our gardener of many years.

Whittier was badly hit by an earthquake in 1987, causing the house to shift off its foundations. When the house was repaired and ready for sale, Bill moved to Prescott, Arizona, one of the places he had visited on an Elderhostel. Here he took college classes every semester, including classes on classical guitar. He served as a docent at three museums. He joined a soaring club that flew every weekend, and went fishing at the lake at Prescott. At the Prescott outdoor park, he taught children about the plants and animals. He was featured in a Prescott documentary. Walmart saw the documentary and took a clip for an advertisement. Bill was paid for his cameo every time the ad aired.

When Bill had a bowel resection for cancer in 2003, his life changed drastically, as he had no bowel control. He gave up all of his out of the house activities but kept up with his interests through magazines. He was fascinated by many things. I found out just how many things he was involved in only after his death in April 2014. He had an enviable dye cast car collection and a gun collection, as well as a rock collection. He was a contributor to the tome on the Brink genealogy. He was a member of the Arizona Magna Carta Barons, the NRA, Soaring Society, Ex-POW Society, and so on.

When Bob graduated from high school in 1949, he decided to go to Fullerton Junior College. I don't remember his major field of study, but he had a good time. Like Bill, he joined the air force (1951) but spent his entire four years stateside. Like Bill, he went to Whittier College for both his bachelor's (1960) and master's (1965) degrees. Auntie Mable was his thesis adviser.

After his discharge, Bob went to Mexico City to study at the University of Mexico. The highlight of that year was getting a job as a movie extra and meeting his idol, Errol Flynn, who was filming *The Sun also Rises*. I can imagine how Errol Flynn must have felt to be greeted by a man six feet four inches tall saying, "You were my hero when I was a little boy." He came home with a full beard.

Bob married Barbara Mathison in 1957. They had three children: Robert Arlington II (1958), Jennifer Anne (1962), and John William (1963). Bob and Barbara divorced, which may have triggered Bob's decision to take the vice principal's job in San Jacinto, California.

Bob taught fifth grade at Lowell Joint School District before accepting the job in San Jacinto, where he served as vice principal (1967–68) and later as principal (1968–79).

A friend of Bob's convinced him to go to Saudi Arabia to work for ARAMCO. The best part of those years (1979–86), other than the salary, were the long vacations, when he could travel anywhere in the world. It was during those years when he was able to go back to Cebu. He was given a wonderful reception by the Aboitiz family, who had been our prewar classmates.

When Bob returned to the States (1986), he settled in Las Vegas, Nevada, where he bought an apartment building and had his own apartment. He remained there until his health deteriorated, necessitating a heart valve replacement. His son, Bob II, moved him to an assisted living facility in Hemet, California. His health never improved after his surgery. He developed a severe intractable infection, which was the cause of his death in December 2013.

When I, Pam, graduated from high school in 1951, I went to Whittier College. I planned to be a nurse, and Whittier offered a bachelor's program for nurses: take the freshman year at Whittier, go to a three-year hospital nursing program, come back to Whittier for the junior and senior years. I did not want to be an elementary school teacher or a secretary. I really wanted to be a matron of an orphanage, but my grandmother explained that I would need a master's degree in social work, and she didn't think I was capable of doing that. Grandmother had tutored me through geometry and knew just how desperately dumb I was at math. That left me with nursing as a profession.

During that first year at Whittier, I learned about a Catholic women's college that was offering a four-year bachelor's program in nursing. I applied and was accepted. The next year, I moved to Mount St. Mary's College in Santa Monica, which was nestled in the hills overlooking Los Angeles. In fact, on a clear day, I could see Catalina Island from the library windows. I don't know when I had been happier than during that first semester. When Mother found out that I wanted to enter the convent, she made me move back home and attend Whittier College. I don't know of a more miserable time in my life than that semester. I pouted the entire time. Mother finally gave in and said I could go back to the Mount, after soliciting my promise that I would not enter the convent until after I finished my degree. I agreed.

That fall, my nursing class of twenty-two was housed in the new nursing residence at St. Vincent's Hospital with the St. Vincent students. We were unique. We attended classes at the Mount on Mondays and Tuesdays and did our clinical ward work from Wednesday to Friday. (All other hospital nursing students had a six-month probationary period of classwork, and then the rest of their two and a half years was spent on the wards five days a week.)

We maintained that schedule through all our specialty rotations, such as pediatrics and psychiatry.

When I graduated in 1956, I took a job at St John's Hospital in Santa Monica on the evening shift, where I met Eric T. Yuhl, MD, a neurosurgeon. He offered me a job as his office nurse with an eye to training me as his permanent surgical nurse. (That never happened.) During that year, an old friend from Whittier told me about his graduate work at Catholic University and suggested I apply. I did and was accepted with a government grant. (When I was accepted, I visited my grandmother to tell her about it. She was surprised to hear that nursing had become respectable enough to be offered at colleges and universities. Her idea of nursing was bedpans and broom closets.)

In 1957, I began graduate studies in psychiatric nursing at Catholic University, where the clinical work was at St. Elisabeth's Hospital in Washington, DC, as well as at the Seton Institute in Baltimore.

In 1959, following my graduation from Catholic University, Mother came to DC. We became tourists. Mother wanted to see everything, especially the Supreme Court. Liz Conaty, a friend I had met, took us to Williamsburg, Mount Vernon, and Monticello in her red and white 1956 Chevy convertible. From DC, we flew to Boston, where we were met by Auntie Mabel's editor. He graciously toured us around town and to all the major tourist spots. From Boston, Mother and I flew to Cincinnati, where we visited with Jane Afleck and her husband, Dave, who was still working for Proctor & Gamble. On that trip, Mother and I also visited Virginia Johnson at the family manor—the Big House. Her husband, Johnny, had died, and her two girls were living elsewhere.

I took a job at the Norwalk State Mental Hospital, where I was assigned to night duty on a medical ward. The only other nurse with a master's degree was the director of nursing. Not being able to get a transfer to day duty, I quit and took a job at the Brentwood Veterans Hospital, where I stayed till Liz Conaty called and invited me to join her in Cincinnati. That sounded like fun, so I applied to the University of Cincinnati for a teaching position, and thinking I had the job, moved to Cincinnati. (Six months later, I was a bridesmaid at Liz's wedding.) It turned out I did not have the university job, so I took a position at the university psychiatric pavilion. Eventually, I was hired as a lecturer at the College of Nursing. During that time, I took a course on Introduction to Anthropology. I fell in love with anthropology.

One day I saw a notice for government-funded doctoral programs for nurses in five fields of study. One of those fields was anthropology. I immediately applied to the Boston University School of Nursing, took the Graduate Record Exams and was accepted. I moved to Boston.

I loved studying anthropology. Loved my teachers. For my doctoral field research, I was interested in either China or Latin America but was told the grant was limited to the continental United States, so I chose Native Americans as my major field of study. (I later found that the committee in charge of the grant gave me a special dispensation to leave Boston and do my field work with the Northern Paiute in Nevada.) During those years in Boston, I spent one summer in Johnson County, Kentucky, learning to do ethnography.

I got a job at UCLA when I finished my doctorate in 1969. Not only was UCLA a wonderful experience, but the Western Conference for Higher Education in Nursing (WCHEN) was one of the most superb opportunities for cross-university collaboration I have ever experienced. Not only did we have seminars to discuss educational issues, especially graduate education, we held annual research conferences with presenter/discussant. Because of the people I met, I founded a nursing research journal (*Western Journal of Nursing Research*) using many of the WCHEN colleagues as associate editors. Those years were a time of growth and excitement in nursing.

In 1982, I was invited to the University of Iowa as a visiting professor and decided to stay. Iowa City is one of the best hidden secrets in the United States, a wonderful place to live.

A former colleague and a coauthor from UCLA, Marilynn Wood, had accepted the position of dean of the faculty of nursing at the University of Alberta, in Canada. She called and offered me the job of associate dean of research. I agreed and began my new career in 1988.

Teaching at a Canadian school introduced me to international nursing research conferences. Perfect! Between the Society of Applied Anthropology conferences, annual meetings of the editors of nursing journals, and nursing research conferences, I was able to travel to places I never would have seen otherwise. I also had the fun of being able to instigate a master's program in nursing at the University of Ghana. Being the research dean allowed me to meet and negotiate with many people for many research endeavors: a very satisfying position.

Mandatory retirement was still in effect when I retired from the University of Alberta in 1998. It was hard to wind down and give up many of the projects that were meaningful and absorbing. The hardest was giving up my editorship of the *Western Journal of Nursing Research*. The publisher wanted an editor who lived in the United States. I finally understood why my mother had such difficulty adjusting to a lack of stimulus. I have managed, however, to find many things to interest me and keep me occupied and am grateful for the time I now have to ride my hobbies without guilt.

I am the last of my nuclear family. I am alone. There is no one left who remembers.

Robert Arlington Brink II, Robert Arlington Brink, John William Brink, Pamela Jane Brink, November 2009. The last time we three were together.

Notes

1. This memory seems distorted. If we were living in Pasadena, we could not have "driven across country." Since Pasadena is in California, we would have simply driven across the state. We did make a cross-country trip when I fell out of the back seat of the car. I was about three years old at the time, so it would have been 1937. I also wonder about the car. My father liked to go to Detroit to buy his cars directly from the manufacturer. Our last car was a seven-passenger Lincoln Zephyr.

2. Mr. Hessenbergher was a Jewish refugee. When the boatload of Jewish refugees landed at Cebu, everyone who could was asked to give them jobs. Mother took Mr. Hessenbergher, as he said on his entry form that he had been the manager of a store. Mother needed help running the store, so she hired him. It turned out he had no more experience at running a store than she had.

3. See the letter by Maude Brink about this school requirement in the appendix.

4. Bob's description of the car we used to drive from Montalongon to Cebu City differs from Bill's description. Since Bill was older and was fascinated by cars, I suspect his account is the correct one.

5. This story about Gerry is directly contradicted by my brothers but was the story my mother told me.

6. This was the story Mother told me about what happened to Dr. Hawk and Morrie Cleland, among others.

7. I am not sure Bob has the correct date or if he is referring to a different consular departure. A letter dated September 7, 1942, was sent by Mrs. Alex A. Brown [nee Lucy Wislizenus, daughter of Mrs. Wislizenus] to my aunt, and describes her departure.

8. See the letter from Mrs. Alex A. Brown/Lucy Car Wislizenus to Mabel Rice, listing the Cebu internees and the living conditions at the junior college.

References and Resources

Books

Anthony, Arthur. *Deliverance at Los Baños: The Dramatic True Story of Survival and Triumph in a Japanese Internment Camp.* St. Martin's Press, 1985.

Hartendorp, A. V. H. *The Santo Tomas Story* (Edited from the official history of the Santo Tomas Internment Camp by Frank H. Golay, with a foreword by Carlos P Romulo.) New York: McGraw Hill, 1964.

Henderson, Bruce. *Rescue at Los Baños: The Most Daring Prison Camp Raid of World War II.* Harper Collins, 2015.

Johnson, Forrest Bryant. *Hour of Redemption: The Heroic WWII Saga of America's Most Daring POW Rescue.* AOL Time Warner. 1978, 2002. (Bataan)

Monahan, Evelyn M. and Rosemary Neidel-Creenie. *All This Hell: U.S. Nurses Imprisoned by the Japanese.* University Press of Kentucky, 2000.

Powell, Laurel Shanafelt. *A Brink Book (& Terpenning).* Powell-Shanafelt Family History Books, 1996.

Pratt, Caroline Bailey, ed. *Only a Matter of Days: The World War II Prison Camp Diary of Fay Cook Bailey.* Bennington, Vermont: Meriam Press, 2006.

Sides, Hampton. *Ghost Soldiers: The Forgotten Epic Story of World War II's Most Dramatic Mission.* New York: Doubleday, 2001. (Bataan)

Stainbrook, Donna. *Our Place in Rural America: Milltown, South Dakota.* 1996. (Available through the author at 27323 419th Ave. Parkston, SD 57366–5812).

Ward, Geoffrey C., and Ken Burns. *The War: An Intimate History: 1941–1945.* Knopf, 2010.

Websites

Burns, Ken. *The War*, a TV series from PBS, can be found for sale on many sites as well as on YouTube. http://kenburns.com/films/war/.

Other books on the Los Baños rescue can be found on Amazon.com. http://www.amazon.com/Deliverance-Los-Banos-Dramatic-Internment/dp/0312191855.

Many photographs can be found on Google of Santo Tomas and the rescue of the internees at Santo Tomas and Los Baños that are in the public domain. See "Santo Tomas prison camp Manila" or "Los Baños Prisoner of War Camp."

https://www.google.com/search?q=santo+tomas+prison+camp+manila&rlz=1C2EODA_enCA546CA547&tbm=isch&tbo=u&source=univ&sa=X&ei=oUvNUor0CuS02AWQwoHQBA&ved=0CGUQsAQ&biw=1032&bih=616.

Gopal, Lou. *Manila Nostalgia.* www.manilanostalgia.com, a blog site containing an article on the Los Baños Internment Camp rescue with photographs and a film clip. The article was written in 2015 in honor of the seventy-fifth anniversary of the rescue. http://www.lougopal.com/manila/?p=2844 Lou Gopal has granted me permission to use the photos on his website.

Beaber, Herman. *Deliverance it has come. A POW Diary.* This blog site contains many links to other stories as well as photographs, including a roster of the navy nurses at Los Baños and a link to the American Ex-POW organization. http://ithascome.bravehost.com/.

Mansel, Roger. An extensive data base of information about prisoners of war in the Pacific during World War II. http://www.mansell.com/pow-index.html.

YouTube. Film clips of the rescues at Los Baños and Santo Tomas are freely downloadable at the Internet Archive. U.S. Army Air Forces "Combat Subjects" # 3274 footage of the Los Baños raid. National Archives Identifier 4854 https://www.youtube.com/watch?v=VINyM3SoFkA.

The website containing the memoir of Claire Wislizenus can be found here: www.rkeller.com.

Documentation

Former Flintville Woman Lived In Cebu Burned by Japanese

Listed with the lost, the former Miss Maud Rice, Mrs. Myron Brink, formerly of Flintville, 12 miles northwest of Green Bay, is reported along with her family, to be among the residents of the city of Cebu in the Philippines which was burned by the Japanese in retaliation for guerrilla activities.

Mrs. Brink's mother and sister have not heard from her since a week before the attack on Pearl Harbor. Mr. and Mrs. Brink lived in the city of Cebu on the island with their three children, two boys and a girl, Pat, who is now about seven or eight years old.

In Cebu she has been a member of a partnership in the operation of a Ten Cent store. Mr. Brink is working with an American firm in the copra business and was president of the chamber of commerce there.

Married in Philippines

In her last letter to relatives here in the United States, Mrs. Brink wrote that she and her family were in no danger and that all arrangements had been made for the protection of women and children during air raids. Since that was before Pearl Harbor, however, Mrs. Brink had no idea that the island would be captured.

Mrs. Brink, tiring of the monotony of every day school life, and being of adventurous spirit, went to the Philippines when she obtained a position as intructor in a Normal school there. She was eventually made a supervisor of English of a number of the private schools on the islands and then married Myron Brink who had also gone out there as a teacher. Later he was employed as superintendent of an English copra concern and then in an American firm.

Relatives and Friends Here

The former Miss Rice was born in Flintville and spent the early part of her life there. Later her family moved to Stevens Poir where she was graduated from Stevens Point Teachers co' and entered on a teaching caree. After teaching at Edgerton and one or two other cities she taught for some years at West Allis before she went to the Philippines.

Mrs. Brink has several relatives and friends in Green Bay, Oconto Falls, Marinette, and the vicinity.

Mrs. Brink's mother was head of the department of mathematics in the Marinette High school for 14 years but resigned a year ago this June. She is now living with another daughter who is Dean of Education at Whittier colle Whittier, Calif.

Newspaper Article stating Maude Brink was Dead

BRINK'S PESETA STORE
75 N. CARMELO ST.
CEBU, CEBU. P. I.

Nov. 27, 1939.

Dear Mabel;

I told you in my last letter that I was sending you
a package for Allan, and that I was sending you the money to
pay for mailing it to him. I had a money order sent, and my
office girl did too much thinking so sent the money order to you
from the P.O. I wanted her to send it air mail, so you would have t
the money before you had to mail the package. Anyway you will have
five dollars when it gets there.

I have been a terrible letter writter for so long.
You must be used to it by now. I suppose you know now whether you s
are going to have your other operation this vacation. How is your
eye now. It seems so long since we have heard from you. or Mother
either.

Our boys are getting so big. Billy is quite a boy.
Bob and Pam have both grown an inch since last summer. They all
seem older, and a lot easier to handle. Billy is doing a lot better
in school these days, and we ha3 think that he has finally grown up.
He is taking his finals in Ancient history. It is very hard. He and
Myron worked all week end on it. When Myron first started to help
him he said,"Why this is so interesting I should think you
would remember it". But I noticed last night that Myron coudn't rem
ember who they were either. There are about twenty Greek names, and
he has to tell who he was and what he did for the world. After fou r
days of it, the only one I remember is King Philip, and that
he was twenty when he went to the thrown, and was 32 when he died.
Billy knows that much and a little more. The only reason that I rembe
remember him is that he is the only one who didn't have a Greek name.

They all take Spanish twice a week, and are doing well in
it. Pam gets 100 every month. She is the best of the lot. Their teach
Miss Mesa, speaks very little English. She says," Billy knows too wel
English, Bob,he cares not to work so hard, but Pam,(here she kisses
the air) Pam she is perfectly!!

She taught them to sing: Are you sleeping brother John.
They sing it all over the place. Pam speaks like a Spaniard.
I would like to have Pam take piano lessons next year. She is taking
dancing now. But I think that paino is more important. Billy still
can not carrey a tune. but Bob is very good.

I have a sewing girl coming today, and want to go and
get some material for Pajamas for all three children. Pam is out.

I wrote you that we were going to pay the insurance didnt
I ? I forget what I wrote before.

I want to get this off in todays mail so will stop and
send it tothe PO.

Love from us all,

Maude

Maude Brink Letter 1939

BRINK'S PESETA STORE

75 N. CARMELO ST.
CEBU, CEBU, P. I.

Nov. 27, 1939

Dear Mabel,

I told you in my last letter that I was sending you a package for Allan, and that I was sending you the money to pay for mailing it to him. I had a money order sent, and my office girl did too much thinking so sent the money order to you from the P.O. I wanted her to send it air mail, so you would have the money before you had to mail the package. Anyway you will have five dollars when it gets there.

I have been a terrible letter writer for so long. You must be used to it by now. I suppose you know now whether you are going to have your other operation this vacation. How is your eye now. It seems to long since we have heard from you, or Mother either.

Our boys are getting so big. Billy is quite a boy. Bob and Pam have both grown an inch since last summer. They all seem older and a lot easier to handle. Billy is doing a lot better in school these days, and we think that he has finally grown up. He is taking his finals in Ancient history. It is very hard. He and Myron worked all weekend on it. When Myron first started to help him he said, Why this is interesting I should think you would remember it: but I noticed last night that Myron couldn't remember who they were either. There are about twenty Greek names, and he has to tell who he was and what he did for the world. After four days of it, the only one I remember is King Philip, and that he was twenty when he went to the throne, and was 32 when he died. Billy knows that much and a little more. The only reason that I remember him is that he is the only one that didn't have a Greek name.

They all take Spanish twice a week, and are doing well in it. Pam gets 100 every month. She is the best of the lot. Their teacher, Miss Mesa, speaks very little English. She says, "Billy knows too well English,

Bob cares not to work too hard, but Pam (here she kisses the air) Pam she is perfectly!"

She taught them to sing: are you sleeping brother John. They sing it all over the place. Pam speaks like a Spaniard. I would like to have Pam take piano lessons next year. She is taking dancing now, but I think that piano is more important. Billy still cannot carry a tune, but Bob is very good.

I have a sewing girl coming today, and want to go get material for Pajamas for all three children. Pam is out.

I wrote you that we were going to pay the insurance didn't I? I forget what I wrote before.

I want to get this off in today's mail so will stop and send it to the PO.

Love from us all,
Maude

Sept. 6, 1941

Dearest Mother and Mabel;
        I have been receiving your letters every week, and they are so interesting right now, all about your trip. When you get this you will have gone and returned to your new house in L.A. I do wonder just where you are going to live. I have read all about the house and it sure sounds nice to me. all but the old climbing up stairs. That isn't so good. I hate to climb stairs.
        Before I go any farther I want to tell you that there is nothing to worry about about me. I am in very good health right now. In fact the best I have been in in many years. It did take me a long time for ,me to get over this last operation. Now I am over it and am just fine. I asked Myron this morning if he didn't think that I am fatter than I have been in years and he said no, I dont! I weigh 130, and I know I look better. My cheeks arn't so hollow. I really thought that I had a cancer, and had about two years to live. It took a lot out of me. Now my mind is at rest so I will put on weight soon now. You went through the same thing when you were my age mother, and you will understand what I have been thinking for so long. I am sure I will never let it bother me again, But being me, I suppose I will act the same way again. We didn't get that report back from the "ayos until the last of May. I thought Myron had recd. it and wasn't telling me. I hated Montelongon, and still do. The nights there were so bad when I was alone. You know I was up there last Nov. when the children had the measles and Billy almost died and I was there alone with him. One day He lay in a coma from eight till three. The only way I could tell he was alive was by touching him, and I'd sit for a long time watching him just dreading to put my hand on him for fear of finding him cold. At three he came out of it.
        We have a chance to sell the place and I want to sell it.
        Pam has a fever today. She seems to be getting an abcess in her ear, and has some fevver. Myron is reading to her, The boys have gone to Lilian to swim with the Melanies. I have just finished changing the furniture around in the Sala. Everytime the place looks as tho it needs a good cleaning I call all of the servents and change everything around. Myron comes home and likes it. There is one thing he always likes me to change things around.I wish I had a real library here. I have so many books thanks to you two, and no good place to put them. When we have a house of our own we are going to have a library.We have four bookcases about the size of the one Mother had in Marinette in the Sala, one in the boys room, and one in Myrons room, and one on the porch. Thanks to you two, we have the finest childrens' library in the P.I. I have sent some of the to the school for suplimentary use.
        Our house is very nice. It has just three bedrooms. The people who lived here before us took out a partition and threw the fourth room into the sala. It makes our sala nice, but we need the other bedroom. for the rooms are small. Myron and I have each a double bed. One room is too small for the two beds. So I have mine in Pams room. and have

Maude Brink September Letter 1941

BRINK'S PESETA STORE

75 N. Carmelo St.
Cebu, Cebu, P.I.

Sept. 6, 1941

Dearest Mother and Mabel;

I have been receiving your letters every week, and they are so interesting right now, all about your trip. When you get this you will have gone and returned to your new house in L.A. I do wonder just where you are going to live. I have read all about the house and it sure sounds nice to me. All but the climbing up stairs. That isn't so good. I hate to climb stairs.

Before I go any farther I want to tell you that there is nothing to worry about me, I am in very good health right now. In fact the best I have been in many years. It did take me a long time for me to get over this last operation. Now I am over it and am just fine. I asked Myron this morning if he didn't think I am fatter than I have been in years and he said no, I don't! I weigh 130, and I know I look better. My cheeks aren't so hollow. I really thought I had cancer, and had about two years to live. It took a lot out of me. Now my mind is at rest so I will put on weight soon now. You went through the same thing when you were my age Mother, and you will understand what I have been thinking for so long. I am sure I will never let it bother me again, but being me, I am sure I will act the same way again. We didn't get that report back from the Mayos until the last of May. I thought Myron had recd it and didn't tell me. I hated Montalongon, and still do. The nights there were so bad when I was alone. You know I was up there last Nov when the children had the measles and Billy almost died and I was there alone with him. One day he lay in a coma from eight till three. The only way I could tell he was alive was by touching him, and I'd sit for a long time watching him just dreading to put my hand on him for fear of finding him cold. At three he came out of it.

We have a chance to sell the place and I want to sell it.

Pam has a fever today. She seems to be getting an abscess on her ear, and has some fever. Myron is reading to her. The boys have gone to Liloan to swim with the Melanies. I have just finished changing the furniture around in the Sala. Every time the place looks like it needs a good cleaning I call all of the servants and change everything around. Myron comes home and likes it. There is one thing he always likes me to change things around. I wish I had a real library here. I have so many books thanks to you two, and no good place to put them. When we have a house of our own we are going to have a library. We have four bookcases about the size of the one Mother had in Marinette in the Sala, one in the boys room, and one in Myron's room and one on the porch. Thanks to you two we have the finest children's library in the P.I. I have sent some of the books to the school for supplementary use.

Our house is very nice. It has just three bedrooms. The people who lived her before us took out a partition and threw the fourth room into the sala. It makes our sala nice, but we need the other bedroom, for the rooms are small. Myron and I have each a double bed. One room your room somehow.

We have a very nice kitchen, with a store room off it that is large, and has room for all the extra cupboards. A large front porch runs all across the house, and has an imposing double stairs rising from the ground and meeting at the top. The house is 14 ft off the ground and has a concrete basement below, double car garage, and servants quarters, and lots more room. The boys have fixed up a club room down there. An airplane club. They spend all their time making planes that fly. But they seem to have the most fun building them. As soon as they finish one they go down town to buy another. We sell them in our store.

We have three very nice children. I spent a week at Del Monte last week with Anita Crawford. I go down there every year for a week. This time I took Pam with me. She was so thrilled at going and had a great time. She didn't miss any school for they teach the same system and Pam carried on from there. Wasn't that nice? When I got back Friday Bobby had some sores on his legs. I fixed them for him and when I had finished, he said; "Thank you Mom, gee you are good to me." Wasn't that sweet?

Saturday morning both boys had to go to the dentist, and Pam is to the doctor about her ear, and Bob about the sores on his leg. Now they are finished with the dentist for a while. All three of them. That's the worst of all. Bobby has a fit every time the dentist works on him. He is just scared to death. Billy and Pam are fine, and have had a lot of work to be done each time than Bob.

Myron is much better this week. He is very tired, and does need a rest.

It has been harder to write this year than ever. I haven't known from day to day whether we would have to go home. Now we won't be able to go home so that is settled for us, and in a few days now we will know whether Japan intends to fight. The second American ship landed in Siberia last night. Japan says that wasn't confirmed and Germany says it is an out and out lie. But we say it landed and Japan hasn't started the fireworks as yet. We are all feeling very cheerful about it today.

The U.S. has sent American soldiers all over the P.I. to muster the P.I. army into the U.S. army. Five hundred were sent out of Manila last week. Cebu got 50 of them. They have been sent way up into the mountain provinces. The Am soldiers are kicking like everything too they think they are being picked on. I haven't much patience with them. I was sent to Laog once and I didn't kick either.

I sure ramble on and on we are living again as tho there were no signs of war any place around. I am so glad we have settled down again; we were up in the air for so long.

I hope you had a lovely trip, and I know the plane didn't hit the Mt Mabel.

Love from us all.
Maude

Appendix d

Letter about Cebu Internees written by Lucy
Brown sent to Mable Rice in 1942

[To my knowledge, this is the only document listing the
Internees at Cebu. Author has the original letter.]

November 25, 1942

Dear Friends of Cebu people:

The enclosed letter from Lucy Brown arrived yesterday. The postmark was
blurred - probably intentionally - and it was impossible to determine whether
it was mailed from East Africa or London but probably it was the East Africa
letter of the two she mentions. It had been opened and passed by the censor.
Not a thing had been cut out so Lucy did a marvelous job in writing within the
rules of censorship. Perhaps there is something to be read between the lines.
What can we do other than reach the International Red Cross?

Our college facilities are being used to duplicate this letter. This is
the first thing that my mother and I have been able to do for our Cebu people
and though it is very little we are glad for the opportunity. We hope there
will be more communications from them to distribute. Lucy's note to me follows
on this page.

Very sincerely yours,

Mabel F. Rice

Mabel F. Rice
Director Elementary Education
Whittier College
(Sister of Maude Brink)

MFR:cd

Mrs. Jennie A. Rice
617 East Philadelphia Street
Whittier, California
(Mother of Maude Brink)

C O P Y
(Lucy's note)

Lourenço Marques, Portuguese East Africa
September 7th, 1942

Dear Mabel:

I shall mail this from here, and send another copy by air mail from England,
"just in case"---. Maude says your mother will mimeograph and mail it to the
people whose names and addresses follow. I think it would be well to make a number of extra copies, too, in case I think of other people who should have them.
But don't let them get in circulation beyond this list.

You are one of those who can and must take up this undertaking to get help
to them. Understand that it must be told only to people who will act, not talk.
We are so afraid of the possible repercussions of ill-advised publicity.

Lucy Brown Letter re Cebu Internees 1942

Let me assure again that the Brinks are all O.K., doing their own part and helping others as well. They'll all pull through; it will be hard, but they'll do it.

Let me hear from you, please. I have added to the addresses given me some of my own friends to whom I have not time to write in such detail. Will you also please send them a copy, with an explanation of how it comes to them?

(Signed) Lucy

Mrs. Alex A. Brown
%Mrs. H. A. Cox
824 Nell Gwynn House, Sloan Ave.,
London, S. W. 3, England

COMMUNICATION

Lourenço Marques, Portuguese East Africa

To Relatives and Friends of My Friends in the Philippines:

I am Lucy(Mrs. A. A.) Brown, resident of Davao, P.I., former resident of Cebu, P.I., and daughter of Mrs. Wislizenus, who is still there. I left Cebu on June 13th, on British-Japanese diplomatic exchange, as Ack was British Vice-Consul in Davao.

I am happy to say immediately that I have no bad news for any of you, and in cases where I have little information, please believe that I have good reason for assuring you that "all well" can be assumed.

I am writing from Lourenço Marques, where the exchange is taking place. This is the first opportunity to write, although we left Manila on June 17th--Japanese censorship, etc., in Shanghai, where we spent about five weeks.

It will probably be best to give you a short synopsis of events in Cebu. Although it will necessarily be written from my own experience, you may take it that mine was typical. Then I shall mention each individual concerned, with some small note about him. When it was known that I was leaving, everyone of course asked me to write to relatives. I couldn't take letters, so this is the best I can do. Maude Brink suggested that I send letter and addresses to her mother, who will mimeograph and mail it to each of you.

One word of warning, which you all MUST heed: DO NOT give your copy to newspapers, etc. Full accounts are being given to proper official quarters--i.e., State Department, International Red Cross, Foreign Office. It requires more discretion than we feel we have, to decide when publicity may help or seriously harm those who remain. Pass on word of their safety, but DO NOT spread details. Here is an example of what I mean: the day we left Shanghai the Japanese-dictated newspapers published a "warning to evacuees" not to spread "false rumours" about internment camps, etc., lest the government be forced to "reconsider its policy." See?

Well -- I was on a visit to my mother in Cebu when the war began. I tried frantically to get back to Davao, but all transportation was taken over by the Army, who told me to stay where I was well off. As Davao was occupied Dec. 20th, they proved quite right! Also, for my mother's sake, it was just as well. We had a couple of tense weeks, most people moving to Busay (the hills overlooking the town). Mom, and I were with the Clelands. I got a short-lived job with the Army; it blew up when the office moved to Mindanao. Before Christmas we had several brief bombings, all directed at Mactan Island, where the oil tanks, etc. are. No hits.

On Christmas afternoon we received an Army order to evacuate to Bogo, at the northern end of the island. It was a mad rush, but we all got started by noon, the 26th. Allister Forbes took us in at the sugar central, in his big house and in other houses in the compound. We stayed there until early in February; during the interim most people got together and built a civilian refugee camp about 20 minutes walk in from the main (north) road, about kilometer 88. Practically all the women and children, and their men, lived there until the invasion, the men going in as often as required, to attend to business requirements.

Just after moving to camp, I got another job, with the Army Transport Service, and continued in it until the end. I stayed at Mom's house in Lahug, with her servants, who, like most of the Filipinos, stood by wonderfully, and spent week-ends with her at Camp 88. Cebu was incredibly quiet all those weeks; actually in the two months I worked there not a bomb was dropped, although we had a number of alarms. There had been two heavy bombings in January, when they got Shell Island and some other oil tanks. During February and March we had three visits from a Japanese cruiser, which shelled the town and the ships in the harbour, damaging only the latter.

It was a queer interim in Cebu, being unharmed, and yet knowing what the end must be. On April 8th there were cruisers reported, and bombers came over after the P-T boats---oh, dear, I must think of the censor! The cruisers went away, but on the afternoon of the 9th, I got a tip that the pay-off was imminent, and that I should be ready to jump. Well, that was no trouble, for I had had a knapsack packed with my few valuables and essentials by my bed all those weeks. I slept with my clothes on and left the house just before dawn, the sky all flame over Opon, where the demolition work had been started. By noon I was safe at the emergency camp at Sudlon, which had been built and stocked by the Army for people working in Cebu. I came part way by car, then took a trail over the ridges. All the way I could hear the explosions from bombing and demolitions; the whole sky was black, and the sun through the smoke was as pale and white as a full moon.

All that day and the next people kept coming in. Sudlon is the heart of the island, in the only remaining bit of forest. It is real jungle--monkeys, wildcats, caves. The houses were all built under complete cover; unfortunately the mess-hall was not, and lots of us were pretty nervous about ganging up there three times a day.

We stayed there a month. It was soon apparent that we would have to "surrender," and be interned. But it was difficult to know how to establish contact with the Japanese, though their planes came over only too often. Things began to come to a head on April 30th, when the camp was bombed and machine-gunned. We had almost an hour of grovelling among the rocks and underbrush; but only two people were hit, neither seriously. A couple of days later, some of us moved up to a cave, well away from the camp clearing, and stayed there, cooking with bats whizzing in and out past our ears, smoking little cigars of native leaf, and eating prodigiously against the presumed lean days of internment. On May 10th, an American prisoner came to the camp with a message, and returned with two of our men to make an offer for us to come in.

We went in on the 12th. We were allowed to have natives to carry our luggage, and to bring in as much as we could get transported of our food stuffs. The latter the Japanese appropriated, but are issuing at least some of it to the camps.

The people from Camp 88 were ahead of us, - came in on May 1st. They were taken to the Provincial Jail, where we also went when we arrived. We were all allowed to keep our personal belongings, except flashlights and a few other things the Japanese wanted for themselves. Things were well organized by the time we got there. A Norwegian ships crew were doing the cooking; water squads supplied the showers and wash-house; Father McCarthy, Myron Brink, and Hector MacLean were the Camp Committee. There was a dormitory for women, a special one (the Dispensary) for mother and children and for older women, and three dormitories for men. (A little euphemism here, as dormitories were actually big cells!) There was the big central yard, where people followed the shade all day. Many of the above arrangements continue in the present camps, especially the American one, which has 105 as against the British with only 25.

On May 16th we were moved--the British to the Lahug Primary School, the Americans and all other to the Junior College. The buildings are only 100 yards apart, but no contact is allowed between occupants. I was separated from my mother, having declared myself as British (bad at the time, but fortunate when it came to this exchange!) We had a month there before I left. I was allowed to visit my mother twice for about an hour, early after the move, but then the officer got cold feet about it. Things seemed to be going very well; they had cleaned and arranged every thing, including an outdoor kitchen. Mom and several others are teaching the children (I did it before I began working in town). She and George Ewart play cribbage; there is lots of bridge (it's still Cebu!) and a poker game begins at 1 p.m. sharp. They are fortunate in having a nurse among them (Billie Self). We had her services at the British camp, too, on asking for her. Dr. Ramos, who had attended many Cebu people for years, is allowed to visit both camps, and in addi- tion is a great help in supplying them with meat. In fact, he is the only con- tact the Japanese allowed us to have.

The Americans are fortunate in having some mining men and generally practical people in their camp. The British are much worse off in this respect; they are all office men with little experience elsewhere and not much initiative. I sup- pose they just never were Boy Scouts! However; they get along. There are very few women there, only five, and of them two are elderly.

Just a bit about their situation:
When I left, there was no actual food shortage. They were getting back (issued by the Japanese) the Camp 88 and Sudlon food stocks. But they won't last forever. The fresh food, too, has to be bought with cash. There is the contradictory (and so characteristically Japanese) policy that they must support themselves, and at the same time cannot get any funds beyond that they happened to have in their pockets at the invasion. So some people have money, but many have not, and the total was rapidly decreasing. What happens when it is gone, I don't know. If the Japanese take over their feeding, it will be slim fare -- cornmeal, and little else, I should think. THEY WILL NEED HELP, and SOON. You cannot, obviously, buy a money order, and mail it to them, or send them food. Not only that, but the Japanese put obstacles, to date insuperable, in the way of all agencies. But you can go to the International Red Cross (not the American), and to them you may quote me as saying that the heads of both camps asked me to report to them that there is by now urgent need of money, food, clothing, and medical supplies. I have already reported this to a very high authority, but not in writing. The problem of getting Japanese permission to send and deliver supplies is extremely difficult, but somehow it MUST be solved. That's their problem; your part is to put the need to them, and to keep on putting it. To those needs I should add "minimum communication," i.e., form post cards, with personal signatures--the "Safe, all well" sort of thing.

One of the contributing factors, true of Cebu as it is not of most places, is the complete destruction of the business part of the city, warehouses, office buildings, shops. It is just a mass of concrete, galvanized iron, and ashes, - most of it done by Army demolition work and resulting fires. It made the Japanese furious, for they got nothing from the town; but the present effect on our people is that they can't get anything either. There is a little feeble electric light now, and a little running water, but very little of either.

I had been interned about a month when I was released. Ack appeared literally from the clouds--by plane en route from Davao to Manila--to tell me about the exchange. I saw him for only five minutes, after a separation of six months, and no word even about each other. But my orders came two days later. I was allowed to spend the night with my mother before I left. Everyone was grand about my going, giving me things I needed, and, best of all, their generous joy in my "escape." May, Virginia, Billie, Carolyn, Peggy all gave me clothes that I simply didn't have. Ack "collected" in the same way at his camp. Our house in Davao was burned on Dec. 23rd, so we had literally nothing of our own. For that matter, we still haven't but everyone has contributed, including the Portuguese and South African Red Cross here, who have been simply wonderful, outfitting me with warm clothes against that English winter which I so dread. Ack hasn't fared so well, as he is so big; though so big as he was, poor thing--lost almost 50 pounds on the camp fare of corn and fruit.

Anyway, I got to Manila, and we are still on the way to England.

Now I'll try to give what you all want: a little gossip about the people who concern you individually. Please forgive me if it is only enough to make you want more. This is something of an undertaking, especially considering that this is my first letter in nine months.

Ray and Imogen Carlson: Were separated in the invasion, and while Mr. Carlson was trying to find his wife, he was taken prisoner. She arrived at the camp, with the children, about a week before we went in, and came up to the cave. She and the children are fine; so is he. They are all together again at the camp.

Ralph Marsden: "Doc" is grand, pinch-hitting as camp cook when required. He was kitchen boss at Sudlon, and I had heated arguments with him over chicken and biscuits. He won.

Billie and Leonard Self: Both fine. Billie is invaluable, of course. She was around right after the Sudlon bombing, to fix up our two casualties, and carries on with all the odd jobs of her profession.

Florence and Phil Sanders: Were at Camp 88, where Florence had their little nipa shack as pretty and immaculate as she did their big house in town. They are at the Cebu camp now, and both fine.

Virginia Chapman: Was hit in the Sudlon bombing--six feet from me. The back of her head was skinned but the skull not touched. Perfectly O.K. She is keeping the topee with the bullet holes in it as a souvenir for her son. She and I were very pally at Bogo, and I shared a shack with them at Sudlon. They are in separate camps now, because of her American passport, but she is fine and gay.

Graham Nelson: Is fine, and cheery, and helpful. He built us an outdoor lean-to kitchen out of galvanized iron and anything else he could find, and made a darn good job of it. He was on my K.P. squad, and I knew he was an experienced dishwasher the first time we worked together; he says that's the way he and his sister do 'em. He got out of Macbate ahead of the Japs, down to Negros, and with two other chaps got a banca (canoe) to try to reach Mindanao. But they were spotted by a cruiser at night, picked up and brought to Cebu. Well treated, no complaint. He's a grand boy.

May and Brooks Roebuck: Were with me in the cave. All their clothes were burned in an army warehouse, but everyone helped them out, as they did me. May and I did much of the cooking in the cave. They were both grand to me; we had fun and certain hardships, and they have been real friends.

Sally and John Heine: Were at Camp 88. John went in a couple of times a week and was fortunately up there when the invasion began. All are well including Margaret.

Lucy and Charlie Goebel: There was talk, before I left, of Lucy's being released on her Swiss citizenship. However, that did not include Charlie, so as far as I know, they are still in. Lucy Ann is well, too.

Marie and Jack Laurence: All well. The children are fine, Gail such a darling.

Maude and Myron Brink: Maude is monitor of her dormitory. Myron's health is better than one would expect. The children are fine. Myron is teaching math to some of the kids. All taking it wonderfully.

Mrs. Doner and daughters: She has been marvelous. She, Mom, and Grace Rigby managed the kitchen while we were at Bogo. Now, I believe, Mrs. Doner teaches some of the kids. I taught Katherine (8th grade) for awhile, and Latin to Jane.

Bob and Grace Rigby: Have taken charge of two-year-old Marcia Pee, whose parents were saved when the Corregidor was sunk. Bobsie is fine, lively as ever.

George Ewart: Hearty and cheerful. Spends hours playing cribbage with my mother. Asks his brother to continue efforts to get money to him.

Mr. and Mrs. Hudson: Were grand to me at Sudlon. It was the cave near their shack where the gang of us took refuge. Mrs. Hudson is a fine little girl, and he is a grand fellow. She could have stayed out of the camp, being a Filipina, but chose to go with him.

Victor McAdam: Hope the cable I sent on arrival here has reached you. Be sure, your mother says, to notify the Mullaneys, and your Uncles Aura and Ray. Both the Mullaneys are O.K., also the children. Your father did perfectly marvelous work for the Army, in the P.R.C. machine shop, making rifle ejectors, machine gun carriages, etc. I heard the highest praise of him from the officer in charge of such things. Your mother and father are both well and both taking it all very pluckily.

Al Fensch: Was at Sudlon, now in Cebu. He stayed over at Mactan through all the bombings but never got a scratch. Very well and cheery.

"Red" Zigler: A newcomer to most of Cebu. He, with Doc Marsden, ran the kitchen at Sudlon. Stayed up in the cave with my gang, and showed us snapshots of his family at Long Beach. The well was blown up by themselves before they left it.

Mary and Morrie Cleland: I wish I could report haveing seen Morrie safe after the invasion. We were allowed no news of the military prisoners, but I feel sure, as well as Morrie was known in Cebu, that we would have heard if he were not O.K. He was invaluable to the Army Transport Service, in which, as I suppose you know, he held a captain's commission. He was with his outfit in the forest beyond Sudlon-- I do know that---and it can be very safely assumed that he came in with the rest for the surrender. We have a hunch that the military prisoners are at the Provincial Jail. Mary is fine, and so are the children. Mary Lou and Margie help her so much, doing laundry and taking care of Maureen, doing a turn on the dish-washing squad,--no grown-up could be better than they are. Dad's house in Opon got a bomb right through the kitchen, this along in January, but he was O.K. The Japanese picked him up when they moved in, asked how old he was, told him to report daily at six p.m. Dad says "Thank you Colonel"---and walks right over to the far side of Mactan and shoves off in a banca, to Bohol, I believe. We all feel sure he is all right; interned, no doubt, but all right.

Martie and Mildred Sands: Mildred was in Manila when war began. She tried to get back on the Corregidor, which hit a mine and was sunk, but she was saved and is interned at Santo Tomas in Manila. I was able to get a message to her from Martie. Martie stayed in Cebu until the invasion, and was at Sudlon. He now puts in his time learning Spanish.

<u>Peggy Ellis:</u> Peggy has matured greatly under a severe trial. Her father and mother were saved from the <u>Corregidor</u>, and I got a message in to Santo Tomas to them. I taught Peggy for awhile (English and Latin) and she used to do my hair and nails. I think the world of her; she's a grand girl. She is studying with my mother now, and helping with the teaching of a couple of the younger children.

<u>Cy Padgett:</u> Doing fine. Stayed in Cebu until the invasion. He and Doc Marsden were the two who went in to make our offer of surrender, then came back to escort us in. How often he has congratulated himself on not bringing Blanche and the children back with him!

<u>Molly Burn:</u> Have not seen her, as she is in Santo Tomas, but received a message asking me to report her as O.K.

<u>Bill Noble:</u> I was able to send Fred a message about Bill. There was a rumour that Bill had been killed. It is <u>not</u> true, and probably originated in the fact that he was injured when a winch broke while military prisoners were loading rice. He had an arm or leg broken, was in hospital and reported improving. You probably did not even know, Suzanne, that he had a commission (Quartermaster, I believe). Fred is O.K., and some people seem to think he was likely to be released from Santo Tomas.

<u>Harriett Richards:</u> Is in Santo Tomas. Looks and feels very well. She rounded up some clothes for me at the camp, and had half an hour's visit with us at the Consulate.

<u>Brownie Wilson:</u> I did not see him, as no one from the Consulate could go to the camp, but I am assured by a man who plays a lot of bridge with him that he is very well and cheerful. I sent him word that I would write to the family.

<u>Col. Edmands:</u> Janie, can you remember far enough back to remember me? I was so surprised to see your husband in Cebu. I wish I could give you late and definite news, but the bit I have may help. I do know that he came through the Cebu invasion safely, for he passed through our forest camp a week later and I saw him for just a moment. We heard soon after that he and his Man Friday, Sergt. Eglewitz, had got over to Negros, and we also heard a speculation that the General had sent him on a mission to Mindanao. This last I do not vouch for. But I do feel that you need have no deep concern for him, except as separation without news is always a matter of concern. I in especial know how you must feel, for I had my own desperate worries from December to June. I suppose your boy is training now; I saw your cable in which you said he had been accepted, and was Papa proud! Let me tell you also, for your own pride, that he did a splendid job in very difficult circumstances, in Cebu. For his kindness to me, in my own rather forlorn situation, I can never be sufficiently grateful. I wish he could know of my tremendous good luck in being re-united with my husband and in getting away. Congratulations, Janie; you have a grand guy.

I cannot promise to carry on a correspondence with all of you. I expect to have a war job, and shall be very busy. But I shall be very gratified to hear from you and to know that my news has reached you. Write:

C/o Mrs. H. A. Cox
824 Nell Gwyn House
Sloane Avenue
London, S.W.3
England

I hope I've made the rounds and not left anyone out. Let me close with the repeated assurance that your folks are O.K., taking a bad break cheerfully, with confidence in a happy ending.

Very sincerely yours,
(Signed)   Lucy Carvell Brown
(Mrs. Alex A. Brown

P.S. (One more item)
Doctor Hawk: Taken prisoner at the military hospital. We have all seen him, and he is all right. Have not seen him since the surrender, but no reason to think any change in treatment. They seem to be very decent to doctors.

(And others)
Mr. and Mrs. Ireland: Joined the bunch at Camp 88, after blowing up everything at the well. They are at the American camp in Cebu now, and want you to know they are all right.
Dave Affleck: Joined Army (2nd Lieut., Q.M.C.) Safe after invasion; without doubt a military prisoner in Cebu.
Earl Baumgardener: Came down from Bataan with a bunch of Navy men. Took charge with Comdr. Grove of the coding section, where I worked. Saw him at Sudlon after the invasion. He and eight other Navy men got away to Negros. They were trying to get to Australia, but I am sure they were too late, and so are sure to be rounded up, either in Negros or Mindanao. R.C.A.: please notify his wife.

****

1. Mr. and Mrs. E. S. Carlson, 4446 Kasson Ave., Chicago, Ill.
2. Walter Marsden, Edgerton, Wisconsin
3. Department of Geology, University of Wisconsin, Madison, Wis.
4. Mrs. Jess Carlson, Monitte, Arkansas
5. Mr. and Mrs. C. P. Sands, 1917 Arlington Ave., Los Angeles, Calif.
6. Col. C. H. Dewey, Med. Corps., General Dispensary, New York City
7. Mrs. Jean D. Nelson, 1364½ Veteran Ave., Westwood Village, Los Angeles, Calif.
8. Miss Florence Burt, Evanston Hospital, Evanston, Ill.
9. Mr. Martin J. Ward, 1120 Rand Terrace, Minneapolis, Minn.
10. Mr. Ray Wilkinson, C/o Telephone Co., Tucson, Ariz.
11. Mr. and Mrs. W. H. Stewart, 317 Charlotte St., Asheville, N.C.
12. Mrs. J. Heine, 420--10th Ave., San Francisco, Calif.
13. Mrs. Jack Kyburz, C/o National Cash Register Co., San Diego, Calif.
14. Mrs. E. R. Laurence, 507 Park Boulevard, Austin, Tex.
15. Mrs. Ralph Sharon, 38 Temple St., Long Beach, Calif.
16. Mr. A. W. Blackburn, Gallipolis, Ohio
17. Mrs. F. K. Doner, Lancaster, Pa., Route 4
18. Mr. Randall Sage, Winnemacoe, Nev.
19. Mr. A. F. Ewart, 2390 Manaau Ave., Honolulu, T.H.
20. Mr. Hudson, Livengood, Alaska
21. Mr. Victor McAdam, 258 W. Colorado, Pasadena, Calif.
22. Ruth Morehart, 150 S. Vista St., Los Angeles, Calif.
23. Mrs. Elizabeth Cleland, R.F.D., #1, East Stanwood, Wash.
24. Mrs. W. M. Zigler, 5665 Lomitas Ave., Long Beach, Calif
25. Mrs. D. W. Williams, Houston, Ohio
26. Mr. V. L. Sanders, 59 Park, Tuckahoe, N.Y.
27. Mrs. William Bevin, 1944--30th Ave., San Francisco, Calif.
28. Mrs. T. M. Jordan, 1197 S. Windsor Boul., Los Angeles, Calif.,
                or
        C/o E. E. Elser
        936 Fremont Ave., Los Angeles, Calif.
29. Mrs. Blanche Padgett, Martinsville, Ind.
30. Mrs. F. M. Noble, C/o Standard-Vacuum Oil Co., 26 Broadway, N.Y.
31. Dr. W. R. Wilson, 328 Dalzell Ave., Ben Avon, Pittsburgh (2), Pa.
32. Mr. and Mrs. David P. Wilson, 7030 Clayton Ave., Dallas, Tex.
33. Dr. Marsh Pitzman, 6 Kingsbury Place, St. Louis, Mo
34. Mr. John Brownlee Wilson, Jr., C/o Mrs. Margaret Eccleston, 42 Morrell St., San Francisco, California

35. Mrs. Margaret Eccleston, 42 Merrell St., San Francisco, Calif.
36. Mrs. Jane Eaton Edmands, C/o War Department, Washington, D.C.
       (Wife of Col. H. J. Edmands, Phil. Scouts)
37. Mrs. Floyd Hawk, C/o U.S. Quarantine Service, Washington D.C.
       (Wife of Dr. Floyd Hawk)
38. Mrs. Fred Tyler, C/o Reed Roller Bitt Co., Ardmore, Okla.
39. Mrs. J. L. Parrott, Claremont, Calif.
40. Miss Ruth Taylor, 26 O'Farrell St., San Francisco, Calif.
41. Mrs. Grace Hagadorn, 450 S. Oakhurst Drive, Beverly Hills, Calif.
42. Mr. and Mrs. Homer Defriest, C/o General Petroleum Co., Los Angeles, Calif.
43. Prof. Carlton Spencer, C/o Law Department, University of Oregon, Eugene, Ore.
44. Prof. Hardin Craig, Stanford University, Calif.
45. Mrs. David Affleck, C/o Proctor and Gamble, New York City
46. R.C.A., New York City (Please forward to Mrs. Earl Baumgardener)
47. Mr. Richard C. Ely, C/o Philippine Bureau, Dept. of the Interior, Wash. D.C.
48. Mrs. Hilma Davies, C/o   "   "   "   "   "   "   "   "   "   "
49. Mr. Arrol Brown, Hingston Ave., Notre Dame de Grace, Montreal, C.Q., Canada
50. Mrs. William Mattas, Ethan, South Dakota #1 (Sister of M. E. Brink)
51. Millard Brink, Parkston, South Dakota
52. Mrs. J. A. Rice, Miss Mabel F. Rice, Whittier, California

159

WHITTIER COLLEGE
Whittier, California

November 25, 1942

Dear Friends of Cebu people:

The enclosed letter from Lucy Brown arrived yesterday. The postmark was blurred – probably intentionally – and it was impossible to determine whether it was mailed from East Africa or London but probably it was the East Africa letter of the two she mentions. It had been opened and passed by the censor. Not a thing has been cut out as Lucy did a marvelous job in writing within the rules of censorship. Perhaps there is something to be read between the lines. What <u>can</u> we <u>do</u> other than reach the International Red Cross?

Our college facilities are being used to duplicate this letter. This is the first thing that my mother and I have been able to do for our Cebu people and thought it is very little we are glad for the opportunity. We hope there will be more communications from them to distribute. Lucy's note to me follows on this page.

Very sincerely yours,

Signed

Mabel F. Rice
Director for Elementary Education
Whittier College
(Sister of Maude Brink)

MFR:ed
Mrs. Jennie A. Rice
617 East Philadelphia Street
Whittier California
(Mother of Maude Brink)

C O P Y
(Lucy's note)

Lourengo Marques, Portuguese East Africa
September 7th, 1942

Dear Mabel:

I shall mail this from here, and send another copy by air mail from England, "just in case" ---. Maude says your mother will mimeograph and mail it to people whose names and addresses follow. I think it would be well to make a number of extra copies, too, in case I think of other people who should have them. <u>But don't let them get in circulation beyond this list.</u>

You are one of those who can and must take up this undertaking to get help to them. Understand that it must be told <u>only</u> to people who will<u> act, not talk.</u> We are so afraid of the possible repercussions of ill-advised publicity.

Let me assure you again that the Brinks are all O.K., doing their own part and helping others as well. They'll all pull through; it will be hard, but they'll do it.

Let me hear from you please. I have added to the addresses given me some of my own friends to whom I have not time to write in such detail. Will you also please send them a copy, with an explanation of how it comes to them?

(Signed) Lucy

Mrs. Alex A. Brown

Mrs. H. A. Cox
824 Nell Gwynn House, Sloan Ave.,
London, S. W. 3, England

COMMUNICATION

Lourengo, Marques, Portuguese East Africa

To Relatives and Friends of My Friends in the Philippines

I am Lucy (Mrs. A. A.) Brown, resident of Davao, P.I., former resident of Cebu, P.I., and daughter of Mrs. Wislizenus, who is still there. I left Cebu on June 15th, on British-Japanese diplomatic exchange, as Ack was British Vice-Consul in Davao.

I am happy to say immediately that I have no bad news for any of you, and in cases where I have little information, please believe that I have good reason for assuring you that "all well" can be assumed.

I am writing from Lourengo Marques, where the exchange is taking place. This is the first opportunity to write, although we left Manila on June 17th—Japanese censorship, etc., in Shanghai, where we spent about five weeks.

It will probably be best to give you a short synopsis of events in Cebu. Although it will necessarily be written from my own experience, you may take it that mine was typical. Then I shall mention each individual concerned, with some small note about him. When it was known I was leaving, everyone of course asked me to write to relatives. I couldn't take letters, so this is the best red I can do. Maude Brink suggested that I send letter and addresses to her mother, who will mimeograph and mail it to each of you.

One word of warning, which you all MUST head: DO NOT give your copy to newspapers, etc. Full accounts are being given to proper official quarters—i.e., State Department, International Red Cross, Foreign Office. It requires more discretion than we feel we have, to decide when publicity will help or seriously harm those who remain. Pass on word of their safety, but DO NOT spread details. Here is an example of what I mean: the day we left Shanghai the Japanese-dictated newspapers published a "warning to evacuees" not to spread "false rumors" about internment camps, etc., lest the government be forced to "reconsider its policy." See?

Well – I was on a visit to my mother in Cebu when the war began. I tried frantically to get back to Davao, but all transportation was taken over by the army, who told me to stay where I was well off. As Davao was occupied Dec. 20th, they proved quite right.! Also, for my mother's sake, it was just as well. We had a couple of tense weeks, most people moving to Bunay (the hills overlooking the town). Mom and I were with the Clelands. I got a short lived job with the Army; it blew up when the office moved to Mindanao. Before Christmas we had several brief bombings all directed at Mactan Island, where all the oil tanks, etc., are. No hits.

On Christmas afternoon we received an Army order to evacuate to Bogo, at the northern end of the Island. It was a mad rush, but we all got started by noon, the 26th. Allister Forbes took us in at the sugar central, in his big house and in other houses in the compound. We stayed there till early February; during the interim most people got together and built a civilian refugee camp about 20 minutes' walk from the main (north) road, about kilometer 88. Practically all the women and children lived there until the invasion, the men going in as often as required, to attend to business requirements.

Just after moving to camp, I got another job with the Army Transport Service, and continued in it till the end. I stayed at Mom's house in Lahug, with her servants, who, like most of the Filipinos, stood by wonderfully, and spent weekend with her at Camp 88. Cebu was incredibly quiet during all those weeks; actually in the two months I worked there not a bomb was dropped, although we had a number of alarms. There had been two heavy bombings in January, when they got Shell Island and some other oil tanks. During February and March we had three visits from a Japanese cruiser, which shelled the town and the ships in the harbour, damaging only the latter.

It was a queer interim in Cebu, being unharmed, and yet knowing what the end must be. On April 8th there were cruisers reported, and bombers came over after the P-T boats===oh, dear, I must think of the censor. The cruisers went away, but on the afternoon of the 9th, I got a tip that the pay-off was imminent, and that I should be ready to jump. Well, that was no trouble, for I had a knapsack packed with my few valuables and essentials by my bed all those weeks. I slept with my clothes on and left the house just before dawn, the sky all flame over Opon, where the demolition work had been started. By noon I was safe at the emergency camp at Sudlon, which had been built and stocked by the Army for the people working in Cebu. I came part way by car, then took a trail over the ridges. All the way, I could hear the explosions from bombing and demolitions; the whole sky was black, and the sun through the smoke was as pale and white as a full moon.

All that day and the next people kept coming in. Sudlon is the heart of the island, in the only remaining bit of the forest. It is real jungle—monkeys, wildcats, caves. The houses were all built under complete cover; unfortunately, the mess hall was not, and lots of us were pretty nervous ganging up there three times a day.

We stayed there a month. It was soon apparent we would have to "surrender" and be interned. But it was difficult to know how to establish contact with the Japanese, though their planes came over all too often. Things began to come to a head April 30th, when the camo was bombed and machine-gunned. We had almost an hour of groveling under rocks and underbrush; but only two people were hit, neither seriously. A couple of days later, some of us moved up to a cave, well away from the camp clearing, and stayed there, cooking with bats whizzing in and out past our ears, smoking little cigars of native lead, and eating prodigiously against the presumed lean days of internment. On May 10th an American prisoner came to the camp with a message, and returned with two of our men to make an offer for us to come in.

We went in on the 12th. We were allowed to have natives to carry our luggage, and to bring in as much as we could get transported of our foodstuffs. The latter the Japanese appropriated, but are issuing at least some of it to the camps.

The people from camp 88 were ahead of us, they came in on May 1st. they were taken to the Provincial Jail, where we also went when we arrived. We were all allowed to keep our personal belongings, except flashlights and a few other things the Japanese wanted for themselves.

Things were well organized by the time we got there. A Norwegian ships crew were doing the cooking; water squads supplied showers and wash-house; Father McCarthy, Myron Brink, and Hector Laclean were the camp committee. There was a dormitory for women, a special one (the Dispensary) for mother and children and for older women, and three dormitories for men. (A little euphemism here, as dormitories were actually big cells;) there was the big central yard, where people followed the shade all day. Many of the above arrangements continue in the present camps, especially the American ones, which has 108 as against the British with only 23.

On May 18th we were moved—the British to Lahug Primary School, the Americans and all others to the Junior College. The buildings are only 100 yards a part, but no contact is allowed between occupants. I was separated from my mother, having declared myself as British (bad at the time but fortunate when it came to this exchange!) We had a month there before I left. I was allowed to visit my mother twice for about an hour, early after the move, but then the office got cold feet about it. Things seemed to be going very well; several others were teaching the children (I did it before I began working in town). She and George Ewart play cribbage; there is lots of bridge (it's still Cebu!) and a poker game begins at 1 p.m. sharp. They are fortunate having a nurse among them (Billy Self). We had her services at the British camp, too, on asking for her. Dr. Ramos, who had attended many Cebu people for years, is allowed to visit both camps, and in addition is a great help in supplying them with meat. In fact, he is the only contact the Japanese allowed us to have.

The Americans are fortunate in having some mining men and generally practical people in their camp. The British are much worse off in this respect; they are all office men with little experience elsewhere and not much initiative. I suppose they just never were Boy Scouts! However, they got along. There are very few women there, only five, and two are elderly.

Just a bit about their situation:

When I left, there was no actual food shortage. They were getting back (issued by the Japanese) the Camp 88 and Sudlon food stocks. But they won't last forever. The fresh food, too, has to be bought with cash. There is the contradictory (and so characteristically Japanese) policy that they must support themselves, and at the same time cannot get any funds beyond what they happened to have in their pockets at the invasion. So some people have money, but many have not, and the total was rapidly decreasing. What happens when it is gone, I don't know. If the Japanese take over their feeding, it will be slim fare – cornmeal, and little else, I should think. THEY WILL NEED HELP, and SOON. You cannot, obviously, buy a money order, and mail it to them, or send them food. Not only that, the Japanese put obstacles, to date insuperable, in the way of all agencies. But you can go to the international Red Cross (not the American), and to them you may quote me as saying that the heads of both camps asked me to report to them that there is by now urgent need of money, food, clothing and medical supplies. I have already reported this to a very high authority, but not in writing. The problem getting the Japanese to send and receive supplies is difficult, but somehow it MUST be solved. But that's their problem; you part is to put the need to them, and keep on putting it. To those need I would add "minimum communication," i.e., form post cards with personal signatures—the "Safe, all well" sort of thing.

One of the contributing factors, true of Cebu as it is not of most places, is the complete destruction of the business part of the city, warehouses, office buildings, shops. It is just a mass of concrete, galvanized iron, and ashes, - most of it done by Army demolition work and resulting fires. It made the Japanese furious, for they got nothing from the town; but the present effect on our people is that they can't get anything either. There is a little feeble electric light now, and a little running water, but very little of either.

I had been interned about a month when I was released. Ack appeared literally from the clouds—by plane en route from |Davao to

Manila—to tell me about the exchange. I saw him for only five minutes, after a separation of six months, and no word even <u>about</u> each other. But my orders came two days later. I was allowed to spend the night with my mother before I left. Everyone was grand about my going, giving me things I needed, and, best of all, their generous joy in my "escape." May, Virginia, Billie, Carolyn, Peggy all gave me clothes that I simply didn't have. Ack "collected" in the same way at his camp. Our house in Davao was burned on Dec. 23rd, so we had literally nothing of our own. For that matter, we still haven't but everyone has contributed, including the Portuguese and South African Red Cross here, who have been simply wonderful, outfitting me with warm clothes against the English winter which I so dread. Ack hasn't fared so well, as he is so bog; though so big as he was, poor thing—lost almost 50 pounds on the camp fare of corn and fruit.

Anyway, I got to Manila, and we are still on the way to England.

Now I'll try to give what you all want: a little gossip about the people who concern you individually. Please forgive me if it is only enough to make you want more. This is something of an undertaking, especially considering that this is my first letter in nine months.

<u>Ray and Imogen Carlson:</u> Were separated in the invasion, and while Mr. Carlson was trying to find his wife, he was taken prisoner. She arrived at the camp, with the children, about a week before we went in, and came up to the cave. She and the children are fine; so is he. They are all together again at the camp.

<u>Ralph Marsden:</u> "Doc" is grand, pinch-hitting as camp cook when required. He was kitchen boss at Sudlon, and I had heated arguments with him over chicken and biscuits. He won.

<u>Billie and Leonard Self:</u> Both fine. Billie is invaluable, of course. She was around right after the Sudlon bombing, to fix up our two casualties, and carries on with all the odd jobs of her profession.

Florence and Phil Sanders: Were at Camp 88, where Florence had their little nipa shack as pretty and immaculate as she did their big house in town. They are at the Cebu camp now, and both fine.

Virginia Chapman: Was hit in the Sudlon bombing—six feet from me. The back of her head was skinned but the skull not touched. Perfectly O.K. she is keeping the topee with the bullet holes in it as a souvenir for her son. She and I were very pally at Bobo, and I shared a shack with them at Sudlon. They are in separate camps now, because of her American passport, but she is fine and gay.

Graham Nelson: Is fine, and cheery, and helpful. He built us an outdoor lean-to kitchen out of galvanized iron and anything else he could find, and made a darn good job of it. He was on my K.P. squad, and I know he was an experienced dishwasher the first time we worked together; he says that's the way my sister and I do 'em. He got out of Masbate ahead of the Japs., down to Negros, and with two other chaps in a banca (canoe) to try to reach Mindanao. But they were spotted by a cruiser at night, picked up and brought to Cebu. Well treated, no complaint. He's a grand boy.

May and Brooks Roebuck: were with me in the cave. All their clothes were burned in an Army warehouse, but everyone helped them out, as they did with me. May and I did much of the cooking in the cave. They were both grand to me; we had fun and certain hardships, and they have been real friends.

Sally and John Heine: were at Camp 88. John went in a couple of times a week and was fortunately up there when the invasion began. All are well including Margaret.

Lucy and Charlie Goebel: there was talk, before I left, of Lucy's being released on her Swiss citizenship. However, that did not include Charlie, so as far as I know they are still in. Lucy Ann is well too.

168

<u>Marie and Jack Lawrence</u>: All well. The children are fine. Gail is such a darling.

<u>Maude and Myron Brink</u>: Maude is monitor of her dormitory. Myron's health is better than one would expect. The children are fine. Myron is teaching math to some of the kids. All taking it wonderfully.

<u>Mrs. Doner and daughters:</u> She has been marvelous. She, mom and Grace Rigby managed the kitchen while we were at Bogo. Now, I believe, Mrs. Doner teaches some of the kids, I taught Katherine (8th grade) for awhile, and Latin to Jane.

<u>Bob and Grace Rigby</u>: Have taken charge of two-year-old Marcia Fee, whose parents were saved when the <u>Corregidor</u> was sunk. Bobsie is fine, lively as ever.

<u>George Ewart</u>: Hearty and cheerful. Spends hours playing cribbage with my mother. Asks his brother to continue to try to get money to him.

<u>Mr. and Mrs. Hudson</u>: Were grand to me at Sudlon. It was the cave near their shack where the gang of us took refuge. Mrs. Hudson is a fine little girl, and he is a grand fellow. She could have stayed out of the camp, being a Filipina, but chose to go with him.

<u>Victor McAdam</u>: Hope the cable I sent on arrival here has reached you. Be sure, your mother says, to notify the Mullaneys, and your uncles Aura and Ray. Both the Mullaneys are O.K., also the children. Your father did perfectly marvelous work for the army, in the P.R.C. machine shop, making rifle ejectors, machine gun carriages, etc. I heard the highest praise of him from the officer in charge of such things. Your mother and father are both well and both taking it very pluckily.

<u>Al Fensch</u>: was at Sudlon, now in Cebu. He stayed over at Mactan through all the bombings but never got a scratch. Very well and cheery.

"Red" Zigler: A newcomer to most of Cebu. He, with Doc Marsden, ran the kitchen at Sudlon. Stayed up in the cave with my gang, and showed me snapshots of his family at Long Beach. The well was blown up by themselves before they left it.

Mary and Morrie Cleland: I wish I could report having seen Morrie safe after the invasion. We were allowed no news of the military prisoners, but I feel sure, as well as Morrie was known in Cebu, that we would have heard if he were not O.K. he was invaluable to the Army Transport Service, in which, as I suppose you know, he held a captain's commission. He was with his outfit in the forest beyond Sudlon—I do know that---and it can be very safely assumed that he came in with the rest for the surrender. We have a hunch that the military prisoners are at the Provincial Jail. Mary is fine, and so are the children. Mary Lou and Margie help her so much, doing the laundry and taking care of Maureen, doing a turn on the dishwashing squad, --no grown-up could be better than they are dad's house in Opon got a bomb right through the kitchen, this along in January, but he was O.K. the Japanese picked him up when they moved in, asked how old he was, told him to report daily at six p.m. Dad says "Thank you Colonel" ---and walks right over to the far side of Mactan and shoves off in a banca! To Bohol, I believe. We all feels sure he is all right; interned, no doubt, but all right.

Martie and Mildred Sands: Mildred was in Manila when war began. She tried to get back on the Corregidor, which hit a mine and was sunk, but she was saved and is interned at Santo Tomas in Manila. I was able to get a message to her from Martin. Martin stayed in Cebu until the invasion, and was at Sudlon. So now puts in his time learning Spanish.

Peggy Ellis: Peggy has matured greatly under a severe trial. Her father and mother were saved from the Corregidor, and I got a message in to Santo Tomas to them. I taught Peggy for awhile (English and Latin) and she used to do my hair and nails. I think the world of her; she's a grand girl. She is studying with mother now, and helping with the teaching of a couple of the younger children.

<u>Cy Padgett</u>: Doing fine. Stayed in Cebu until the invasion. He and Doc Marsden were the two who went in to make our offer of surrender, then came back to escort us in. how often he has congratulated himself on not bringing Blanche and the children back with him.

<u>Molly Burn</u>: have not seen her, as she is in Santo Tomas, but received a message asking me to report that she is O.K.

<u>Bill Nobel</u>: I was able to send Fred a message about Bill. There was a rumor that Bill had been killed. It is not true, and probably originated in the fact that he was injured when a winch broke while military prisoners were loading tice. He had an arm or leg broken, was in hospital and reported improving. You probably did not even know, Suzanne, that he had a commission (Quartermaster, I believe). Fred is O.K., and some people seem to think he was likely to be released from Santo Tomas.

<u>Harriet Richards</u>: is in Santo Tomas. Looks and feels very well. She rounded up some clothes for me at the camp, and had half and hour's visit with us at the consulate.

<u>Brownie Wilson</u>: I did not see him, as no one from the consulate could go to the camp, but I am assured by a man who plays a lot of bridge with him that he is very well and cheerful. I sent him word that I would write to the family.

<u>Col. Edmands</u>: Janie, can you remember far enough back to remember me? I was so surprised to see your husband in Cebu! I wish I could give you late and definite news, but the bit I have may help. I do know that he came through Cebu invasion safely, for he passed through our forest camp a week later and I saw him for just a moment. We heard soon after that he and his Man Friday, Sergt. Eglewitz, had got over to Negros, and we also heard a speculation that the General had sent him on a matter of deep concern. I in especial know how you must feel, for I had my own desperate worries from December to June. I suppose your boy is training now; I saw your cable in which you said he had been accepted,

and was Papa proud! Let me tell you also, for your own pride, that he did a splendid job in very difficult circumstances, in Cebu. For his kindness to me in my own rather forlorn situation, I can never be sufficiently grateful. I wish he could know of my tremendous good luck in being re-united with my husband and in getting away. Congratulations, Janie; you have a grand guy.

I cannot promise to carry on a correspondence with all of you. I expect to have a war job, and shall be very busy. But I shall be very gratified to hear from you and to know that my news has reached you. Write:

c/o Mrs. H. A. Cox, London, England (address withheld).

I hope I have made the rounds and ot left anyone out. Let me close with the repeated assurance that your folds are O.K., taking a bad break cheerfully, with confidence in a happy ending.

Very sincerely yours, signed
Lucy Carvell Brown
(Mrs. Alex A. Brown

P.S. (One more item)

Doctor Hawk: Taken prisoner at military hospital. We have all seen him, and he is all right. Have not seen him since the surrender, but no reason to think any change in treatment. They seem to be very decent to doctors.

(And others)

Mr. and Mrs. Ireland: joined the bunch at camp 88, after blowing up everything at the well. They are at the American camp in Cebu now, and want you to know they are all right.

<u>Dave Afleck</u>: joined Army (2nd Lieut., O.M.C.) Safe after invasion; without doubt a military prisoner in Cebu.

<u>Earl Baumgardener:</u> Came down from Bataan with a bunch of Navy me. Took charge with Comdr. Grove of the coding section, where I worked. Saw him at Sudlon after the invasion. He and eight other Navy men got away to Negros. They were trying yo get to Australia, but I am sure they were too late, and so are sure to be rounded up, either in Negros or Mindanao. R.C.A.: Please notify his wife.

The rest of the letter is a list of the names and addresses of people to whom the letter was to be sent.

Santo Tomas........INTERNMENT CAMP
Manila, ...PHILIPPINES

DATE .August.11,.1943.....

Miss Mabel Rice,
 Whittier College,
  Whittier, California
   U. S. A.
Dear Mabel and Mother:-

          We are all in very good health. Myron had a bad time
for about four months due to high blood pressure but got well after we came
to Manila in December. Billy is 14-1/2 and weighs #115, is 5'-7"; Bob #105,
5'-3"; Pam weighs #80 and is tall for her age. They will have their second
birthdays in camp next month. I have already had mine. I weigh as usual
#130. Billy is a sophomore; Bobby in seventh grade; Pam fifth grade. She
does good work. They all received their first communion in December. They
like it here. They have made many new friends.

          We have built ourselves a bamboo and nipa house 10' X 12' where we spend
the daylight hours cooking, washing and doing home work. I have learned to
cook rice without burning it. We use a charcoal stove for all our cooking.
I make hot cakes of corn, rice, and cassava flour. We use brown sugar for
everything and like it. Coconut milk is very palatable on the morning mush
and in the cooking.

          Our people have remained in good health and in remarkable spirits. We
are all so busy that the weeks and months just fly past. Each internee has a
definite work assignment which requires about two hours per day.

          The camp grounds comprise about 40 acres. There are five large buildings.
One is for a hospital. The others are used for dormitories. Pam and I are
in a room with some of our old friends. The boys are in one room on the third
floor of the same building Myron is in. He is on the first floor to avoid
climbing steps. We are very well entertained by internee talent. We have
football, baseball, boxing (Bob is interested in boxing). We have lectures,
Church services, stage shows and sometimes a movie.

          Please send a copy to Hazel Mattas in Parkston, and tell E. A. Seiden-
spinner, Eldorado Oil Works, 311 California St., San Francisco that you have
heard from us.
                              Love,
                         (Signed) Maude E. Brink
                         Maude Elizabeth Brink

Maude Brink Letter from Santo Tomas 1943

COPY

Santo Tomas ...INTERNMENT CAMP
Manila, ... PHILIPPINES

DATE. August. 11.. 1943..

Miss Mabel Rice
Whittier College
Whittier, California
U.S.A.

Dear Mabel and Mother-

We are all in very good health. Myron had a bad time for about four months due to high blood pressure but got well after we came to Manila in December. Billy is 14 ½ and weighs #115, is 5'7": Bob #108, 5' 3": Pam weighs #60 and is tall for her age. They will have their second birthdays in camp next month. I have already had mine. I weigh as usual #130. Billy is a sophomore; Bobby in seventh grade; Pam fifth grade. She does good work. They all received their first communion in December. They like it here. They have made many new friends.

We have built ourselves a bamboo and nipa house 10' x 12' where we spend the daylight hours cooking, washing and doing homework. I have learned to cook rice without burning it. We use a charcoal stove for all our cooking. I make hot cakes of corn, rice, and cassava flour. We use brown sugar for everything and like it. Coconut milk is very palatable on the morning mush and in the cooking.

Our people have remained in good health and in remarkable spirits. We are all so busy that the weeks and months just fly past. Each internee has definite work assignment which requires about two hours a day.

The camp grounds comprise about 40 acres. There are five large buildings. One is for a hospital. The others are used for the dormitories. Pam and I are in a room with some of our old friends. The boys are in one room on the third floor of the same building Myron is in. he is on the first floor to avoid climbing steps. We are very well entertained by internee talent. We have football, baseball, boxing (Bob is interested in boxing). We have lectures, Church services, stage shows and sometimes a movie.

Please send a copy to Hazel Mattas in Parkston and tell E. A. Seidenspinner, Eldorado Oil Works, 311 California St, San Francisco that you have heard from us.

Love,

Signed Maude E. Brink
Maude Elizabeth Brink

IMPERIAL JAPANESE ARMY

I am interned at Philippine Internment Camp No. 2

My health is — excellent; good; fair; poor.

Message. (Limited to 25 words.)

LETTER RECEIVE

IT FOR ME NEED FOOD AND

CLOTHES FOR ALL SPENT S

ANNIVERSARY LAST WEEK

Signature

SERVICE des PRISONNIERS de GUERRE
俘虜郵便

NAME MYRON E BRINK

NATIONALITY U S A

PHILIPPINE INTERNMENT CAMP NO 2

TO HAZEL V. MA

ETHAN SO. D

12260 U S A

U.S. CENSOR

Myron Brink Card from Santo Tomas no date

From M. E. Brink   U.S.Army Postal Service
Philippine Islands   ...P. ..March 5, 1945

To Mrs Jennie Riceand
Miss Mable Rice
115 Berkeley Way,
Whittier, California.
                    American Red Cross
                                        Feb, 24, 1945

Dear Mother, Mabel and boys:-

          We were rescued yesterday from Los Banos Internment
Camp in the glorious American way. All alive.

          We were absolutely starving and out of food, and had
nothing left unless the Americans came, They did come
at exactly then 7.00 A.M. Billy, Pam and I ran out
when we heard the planes coming over, We thought they were
dropping bombs. Then we saw that the bombs were opening
and parachutes started dropping, The whole camp saw them
We jumped into our ditches and stayed there until we
heard a voice shout," any Japs in there"? We looked up and
there was an American soldier: The Americans had arrived
in the nick of time.

          Myron had been in the hospital with a bad case of

beri- beri since December 20th. He could not get better
without proper food and medicine. In fact, he was getting
worse steadily. The Americans arrived just in time. They
say two weeks will cure him.

          Now, back to yesterday morning. The bullets were
still whizzing around us when word came through,"take
only light hand bags and get to the tanks at once before
Jap reinforcements arrive". We dashed in- I packed
one change for each of us and we walked out of that babboo
shack for ever. We got into the tanks,great iron things
Myron was in another tank. We drove down into the lake
and like a fairy story, simply kept on going right down
into the water- a great iron boat, half way across
the Japs opened fire on us, Our soldiers fired back for
about 20 minutes.

          They got us all out of that camp, to the last man,
loosing only one soldier and about 10 internees wounded,
none seriously, They are very proud of the feat, They
consider it the most important and perfevt so far as
we were all to be massacred at out 7 00 o'clock roll call
two minutes longer would have been too late, We knew
we have lived through a miracle;

          Myron is much better today. Billy is my height
and we both weigh 115 #Bob is 4 inches shorter and wei
105 #. Pam is fine, As soon as thin and up we will
well again. We are all terribl as eye.
never lost our spirits except in

Maude Brink Letter February 24, 1945

From M. E. Brink

U.S. Army Postal Service
Philippine Islands
March 5, 1945

To Mrs. Jennie Rice and
Miss Mabel Rice
115 Berkley Way
Whittier, California

American Red Cross

Feb 24, 1945

Dear Mother, Mabel and boys;

We were rescued yesterday from the Los Banos Internment Camp in the glorious American way. All alive.

We were absolutely starving and out of food, and nothing left unless the Americans came. They did come at exactly 7 a.m. Billy, Pam and I ran out when we heard the planes coming over. we thought they were dropping bombs. Then we saw that the bombs were opening and parachutes started dropping. The whole camp saw them. We jumped into our ditches and stayed there until we heard a voice shout "any Japs around here?" we looked up and there was an <u>American soldier</u>: the Americans had arrived in the nick of time.

Myron had been in the hospital with a bad case of beri-beri since December 20th. He could not get better without proper food and medicine. In fact, he was getting worse steadily. The Americans arrived just in time. They say two weeks will cure him.

Now back to yesterday morning. The bullets were still whizzing around us when word came through, "take only light hand bags and get to the tanks at once before Jap reinforcements arrive." We dashed in – I packed one change for each of us and we walked out of that bamboo shack forever. We got into the tanks, great iron things. Myron was in another tank. We drove down into the lake and like a fairy story, simply kept on going down into the water – a great iron boat. Half way across the Japs opened fire on us. Our soldiers fired back for about 20 minutes.

They got us all out of that camp, to the last man, losing only one soldier and about 10 internees wounded, none seriously. They are very proud of the feat. They consider it the most important and perfect as far as <u>we were all to be massacred at 7 o'clock roll call</u> two minutes longer would have been too late. We know we have lived through a miracle.

Myron is much better today. Billy is my height and we both weigh 115# Bob is 4 inches shorter and weighs 105#. Pam is fine, as soon as we get fed up we will be well again. We are all terribly thin and weak but never lost our spirits except ...

(Brother)
Mr. Millard Brink.
imock, So.Dak.
I am still in the hospital, but picking up fast. the rest of the family are getting plenty of good food and regaining health so noticeably, I didnt know how thin I was till the swelling went down. Some of the people are still horribly bloated but it doesnt look like any more would die. My , we have been marvelously treated. hey have undoubltedly told better than I can our thrilling rescue. It just cant be properly detailed. We hear of so many of our dear friends who have either been murdered or starved in other camps. I dont new our plans beyond getting back to the States some way as quickly as possible. We will go to Maude's people first as they have already got a house arranged for us. I will come East as soon as possible to go to Mayo Brothers. I hope your people are alright.
My family has had a remarkable d elivery and marvelous luck at times when it seemed that all was lost.
I surely hope to see you all together again , but am making no definite plans.

                    Love to all Myron.

Myron Brink Letter March, 1945

Mar, 1, 1945

(Brother)
Mr. Millard Brink.
Imock, So. Dakota

I am still in the hospital, but picking up fast. The rest of the family are getting plenty of good food and regaining health noticeably, I didn't know how thin I was till the swelling went down. Some of the people are horribly bloated but it doesn't look like any more will die.my, we have been marvellously treated. They have undoubtedly told better than I can our thrilling rescue. It just can't be properly detailed. We hear of so many of our dear friends who have either been murdered or starved in other camps. I don't now our plans beyond getting back to the states as quickly as possible. We will go to Maude's people first as they have already got a house arranged for us.

I will come east as soon as possible to go to Mayo Brothers.

I hope your people are alright.

My family has had a remarkable delivery and marvelous luck at times when it seemed that all was lost.

I surely hope to see you all together again, but am making no definite plans.

Love to all Myron

701 Sycamore Drive,
Whittier, Calif.

September 16, 1945.

Dear Hazel:-

Yours of the 7th came yesterday. The first personal
letter to be delivered to our new address.

The kids like their school very much. I like it too for all the
books and equipment are furnished free. Also the transportation.
We are all getting along swell except Maude who tried to catch
Mabel's car when it started to go wild at the curb on a down hill
parking. Both she and Mabel got bumped around but Maude got a
whack on the head that knocked her out and the amount of shin left
on her legs wouldn't cover a humming bird. She was quite ill for
the first day and the next morning but roused up when some of our
Philippine friends surprised us. They just drove in with their
trailer and said we're here. We sure were glad to see them for
we had been very close to them in the Islands and had gone through
internment together. They left the next day for Fresno where his
mother lives. From there he is going back to the P.I. for his company. We have a lot of company here almost like being in the
P.I. Yesterday afternoon while we were having a disch of tea a
lady that has been very nice to us here brought over her husband
who had just got back from Brazil. He is an Army Doctor and should
are very close neighbors. While they were here some other neighbors
came and asked all of us to come over for a barbeque sugger. I was
just washing up the tea things when lo and behold 4 of our Philippine
friends dropped in. Two of them are natives of South Dakota and
very dear friends. They all work at the Philippine Packing Co that
we used to visit on our vacations. I am sure I have told you of the
good times that we had there. They pack the Del Monte pineapples.
They brought some cousins with them and the man told me who to contact
in LA to get some financial help on buying goods to ship out to the
Islands. I don't know what will come of it but I will investigate.

Farm. Confidentially Millard agreed to buy the farm at $30.00 if
I would let him have the crop. I said ok and would knock off $300
to bore a new well. If he can come through with that I will be in
a much better position. Margaret says she has a possible buyer for
my lots in LA and I can borrow on my life insurance policy if necessary. I am still hoping to get something to do that will help
keep the wolf from the door and help pay off debts incurred during
internment. I don't feel that any of my propositions are sound e-
nough to ask you to put money into them but if I do I will send you
a wire and you can let me know how much you can put into them. I
have a proposition here for the manufacture of a toy that looks
good but the inventor that has the patent is inclined to be very
optimistic and I am not too sure that the prospects are as good
as he paints them. Of course the shipments to the P.I. will be
more certain when they get started but nothing has been developed
of a definite nature yet.

As to your visitor. Don't let your pleasures be spoiled by what
others say. If he is a nice fellow and I assume he must be or

Myron Brink Letter September, 1945

sell the farm.

I don't know what your preferences would be but a change in climate is a pick up for any one. If you did come out I might be able to go back with you.

Isn't it just awful to be so upset about everything. Nothing definite and so many blank walls ahead on everything one attempts to do. I don't think you can imagine our predicament. We don't have anything to keep house with. All we brought with us was the clothes the red cross gave. None of that could be worn here but we now have plenty of clothes. We dont have linen tho for beds and stuff like that. And the worst of it is you can't get it. We need enough stuff for five. Fortunately Mabel had extras and we are using them but I will have to go back to the Islands eventually and the family will have to establish housekeeping here some where. No one has anything left in the Islands so I will have to take from here what I need there. One just goes around in circles. If you see any bargains in used materials let me know what they are and the approximate price and maybe we can do some business.

Maude is ironing, the boys are in school(learning to type) Pam is getting ready to combine breakfast and dinner into one meal.

I guess that's all.

Myron.

Myron Letter 1945 Page 2 no date

701 Sycamore Drive,
Whittier, Calif.

September 16, 1945

Dear Hazel: -

Yours of the 7th came yesterday. The first personal letter to be delivered to our new address.

The kids like their school very much. I like it too for all the books and equipment are furnished free. Also the transportation. We are all getting along swell except Maude who tried to catch Mabel's car when it started to go wild at the curb on a downhill parking. Both she and Mabel got bumped around but Maude got a whack on the head that knocked her out and the amount of skin left on her legs wouldn't cover a hummingbird. She was quite ill for the first day and the next morning but roused up when some of our Philippine friends surprised us. We were sure glad to see them for we had been very close to them in the Islands and had gone through internment together. They left for Fresno the next day where his mother lives. From there he was going back to the P.I. for his company. We have a lot of company here almost like being in the P.I. yesterday afternoon while we were having a dish of tea a lady who ad been very nice to us here brought her husband who has just got back from Brazil. He is an army doctor and should [the next line is too obscure to read] are very close neighbors. While they were here some other neighbors came over and asked all of us to come over for a barbeque sugger [sic]. I was just washing up the tea things when lo and behold 4 of our Philippine friends dropped in. two of them are native of South Dakota and very dear friends. They all work at the Philippine Packing Company that we used to visit on our vacations. I am sure I told you of all the good times we had there. They pack the Del Monte pineapples. They brought some cousins with them and the man told me who to contact in LA to get some financial help on buying good to ship out to the islands. I don't know what will come of it but I will investigate.

Farm: Confidentially Millard agreed to buy the farm at $30.00 if I would let him have the crop. I said OK and would knock off $300 to bore a new well. If he can come through with that I will be in a much better position. Margaret says she has a possible buyer for my lots in LA and I can borrow on my life insurance policy if necessary. I am still hoping to get something to do that will help keep the wolf from the door and help pay off debts incurred during internment. I don't feel any of my propositions are sound enough to ask you to put money into them but if I do I will send you a wire and you can let me know how much you can put into them. I have a proposition here for the manufacture of a toy that looks good but the inventor that has the patent is inclined to be very optimistic and I am not too sure that the prospects are as good as he paints them. Of course the shipments to the P.I. will be more certain when they get started but nothing has been developed of a definite nature yet.

As to your visitor. Don't let your pleasures be spoiled by what others say. If he is a nice fellow and I assume he must be or you wouldn't enjoy talking to him go ahead and let him call.

It isn't good to be too much alone and a person who can talk interestingly is always good for jagged nerves and I'm sure yours must be rather raw at times. Don't worry about his being a Catholic. I married one and if I can live with one you should be able to talk to one.

Our furniture mostly isn't ours. The lady we bought the house from left a lot of her stuff here and a friend of ours from Arcadia that sold her house is sending over some pieces for us to look after and use. Our living room furniture we bought new and it looks nice we didn't buy any dining room furniture as we can still eat off our knees if necessary. We are more pleased with our stove every day. Yesterday we found it had salt and pepper shakers on it. We thought they were just ornaments but found out by accident what they were and they were full. We enjoy our refrigerator immensely and don't have any puddles to clean up except in the bath room where one of the bowls leaks. I am getting to be quite a fixer and patched it up with porcelain cement. Only a few drops now and I'll probably be able to give it a real fixing when I can find the little hole.

Frankly I don't see how I can come east till I get something started here and maybe after I get it started I can't get away. Don't look for me till you hear me puffin' down the highway.

Anything that you have to send on to us let it come and we can use it. If you could let us know what you are sending, we wouldn't buy those articles. We'd just wait till yours arrived.

Sincerely,
Signed: Myron
Middie runned away.

Memoir of Claire Wislizenus

By permission of her great-grandson

Sir Robert
Robert Keller
Knight Commander,
Royal and Military Order of Constantine the Great KCRCG

CLAIRE WISLIZENUS
JAPANESE INTERNMENT
1941-1945

Editorial note: *I knew Claire Wislizenus, (1875-1972) my great grandmother, very well during my childhood and into adulthood. To me, she was the most well read and educated person whom I had ever known to that time or since. She wrote out the story of her internment experiences during WWII and typed it out when she was returning to the U.S. I often heard her discuss her internment by the Japanese and to read this account now, many years after her passing, brings a fond remembrance of her sparkling personality. She had many quaint sayings and twists of the English language that were delightful. As I type this account, I can see her face as she would relate these stories of that time. The daughter whom she mentions in the story is her second daughter, Lucy Carvel who married a Brit. Margaret was in San Francisco with her daughter, Valerie during the War. This is my best attempt at interpreting the documents given to me by Valerie Burton, my mom's sister and her granddaughter. I have adjusted the punctuation and tried to correct spelling. Otherwise, I have typed them exactly as given. I have those copies for anyone who may wish to view them. As you read this, remember that it was penned shortly after her release while the sting and pain of over four years of internment were still fresh in her mind. Great grandmother lived thirty years past the end of the War and subsequently had many Japanese friends. However, she hated the Japanese government of the time and the Japanese soldiers who imprisoned her.*

Claire Alterton and Judge Adolf Wislizenus (1864-1926) went out to the Philippines from St. Louis in 1902 where he was to preside over the Court of the First Instance in Cebu, being appointed the first American judge to the Philippines by President [Theodore] Roosevelt. Judge Wislizenus served as judge and jury over a population of one million at the time and decided over both civil and criminal cases as well as probate matters. He had a reading knowledge of French and Italian but found that all cases had to be conducted in Spanish, the court language of the islands. A few months later he wrote out court opinions from the bench, in perfect Spanish. He and

Claire were the center of the local social life and he wrote that his life might have been different but the knowledge he had contributed to justice even in that remote corner of the world had made it all worthwhile. He died from complications from a spider bite Nov. 12, 1926. Claire remained in Cebu until the War.

As related by Claire Wislizenus *(1875-1972)*:

Before I take you behind the lines, so to speak, I should like to give you just a little of the background of all that happened between Dec. 1941 and April 1945.

When I went out to the Philippines in 1902, I almost had to look them up in a geography. Only after my arrival there did I realize how much of historical and romantic interest they held. There are about 7000 islands in the archipelago, with only perhaps 1500 of them inhabited. The earliest inhabitants of the Island were various tribes of Malays who invaded them, each wave of invaders driving the preceding ones farther back into the mountains, until today the only surviving types of those first settlers are found in the remote parts of the Islands among the Negritos of Zambales on the island of Luzon.

In 1521, Ferdinand Magallanes, a Portuguese navigator sailing for the King of Spain landed in Cebu, the island on which I lived for forty years. He made friends with the King of Cebu, who brought in all his people to have them baptized, and in 1941, the spot was still marked by a shrine in the kiosk containing a tall wooden cross, at the foot of which the faithful natives toss the half-burned candles and their precious centavos. Magallanes, or Magellan as we know him, took possession of the island in the name of the King of Spain, and King Tupas agreed to pay tribute to the new claimant to his country. Across the channel from Cebu there lies a narrow half-moon shaped island, now the site of one of the largest coconut oil refineries in the world owned by Lever Bros. The ruler of this small island was made of sterner stuff than was King Tupas of Cebu. He said he was quite willing to trade with Spain on friendly terms, but that he paid tribute to no man. Magellan told him if he refused he would learn what Spanish lances could do. Lapu Lapu replied that his men also had lances. Magellan ordered his Malay sailors to remain in their native boats, and with his Spanish followers, attacked the inhabitants of Mactan. The natives came swarming down to the seashore, and in the fight, Magellan was pinned to the ground by one of their bamboo lances. His men fled in panic to the Cebu side. Magellan's voyage had ended disastrously for him, but his ship returned to Spain under the command of Del Cano, and the first circumnavigation of the globe had been accomplished. Magellan had given the name Mare Pacificum to the ocean we call the Pacific and which so often belies its name. *He had never seen it in a typhoon.*

In 1542 a little more was added to the knowledge concerning the islands when Villalobos, also on a voyage of discovery, gave them the name Philippines in honor of Prince Philip of Spain, but there still were no attempts at settlement. In 1565 Legaspi arrived in Cebu, bringing with him several priests and other settlers. He built the huge fortress, Fort San Pedro, which still guards the entrance to the city of Cebu. In 1571 Legaspi continued his journey to the north and founded the city of Manila, or as Kipling says, "That is another story".

By 1941, 420 years after the landing of Magellan, the city of Cebu had grown into a metropolis of perhaps 75,000 inhabitants, second only to Manila in every respect. We had a splendid harbor, fine schools, great oil installations, beautiful homes, and one of the finest country clubs in the Orient. The oldest street in the Philippines was Calle Colon, or Columbus, with its red tile roofs and stairways hollowed out by generations of footsteps.

In this far-away spot life was very pleasant and profitable until December 8th, 1941, December 7th to you, since we being east of the 180th are a day ahead. There had been the prospect of war with Japan, in the perhaps not too distant future, and military preparations were under way. Quartermaster supplies were arriving daily, Philippine Constabulary soldiers were being intensively trained and a group of American officers had been detailed to Cebu. The general idea was not IF there should be war but WHEN. My daughter, Lucy, who lived in Davao where her husband was one of the leading hemp merchants of the Islands, had arrived in Cebu to spend Xmas with me, and her husband was to join us for the great event of the year, the Christmas party at the Country Club. On Dec. 5th I had about 60 people for a cocktail party, which according to Cebu custom began about six and lasted till midnight. The following night there was another one at the Quarantine Station on a nearby island, and Sunday a round of visitors many of whom had known my daughter as a little girl.

Monday morning, we were getting ready to spend the day up in the hills where several of the Americans had lovely suburban homes. The sound of revelry by night in the Belgian capital the night before the Battle of Waterloo changed to whispers from white lips, "The foe! The foe! They come, they come." Even as were shocked on the morning of the 8th, when my telephone rang at six o'clock bringing the fateful message, "The Japs have bombed Pearl Harbor." I had a class at the university every morning at seven and I went as usual, to find the faculty and students more or less stunned. The next few days passed uneventfully, while many of the students made arrangements to return to their homes on near-by islands. There was nothing we could do but wait.

On the morning of Dec. 14th, about nine o'clock, my neighbor came rushing to the door with the news that the Japs were bombing the ships in the harbor. As he was speaking we could see the first of the bombers, like great silver dragonflies in the lovely clear blue sky. I had a private school of about 150 pupils, and most of them had been present during the anxious week, for their parents felt they were safer at school under the supervision of my excellent staff of Filipino teachers. In about an hour the quarantine doctor came to me and asked if I would turn the schoolhouse over to him for a base hospital, for he knew there would soon be casualties. Everything pertaining to school was taken out with the exception of some tables and chairs which we thought might be of use. Incidentally, I never saw any of them again.

Within a day or two some of the Americans left the city and went to Busay in the hills. Among the 40 or more who went were most of the children in Cebu. My daughter stayed in town and went into the military office decoding radiograms from Gen McArthur. With her was the wife of an Englishman, who by the way has just bought a home in South Laguna. We lived comfortably enough in our evacuation camp although we were pretty crowded. The weather was at its best. Although Mark Twain said that the difference between winter and summer in the tropics is the difference between weather that will melt a brass doorknob and weather that will only make it mushy, the months from November to March are lovely in that part of the islands. From our elevated position we could see the destruction being wrought by the dive-bombers. The few commercial planes, which made Cebu their headquarters, we saw bombed and burned on the field just below us. The three big oil installations on Mactan, Standard, Texas and associated, as well as Shell on another small island, all went up in smoke and flames under repeated attacks of the dive-bombers. Still no Japanese came ashore. We still had our radios, and we knew of the total destruction of our planes on Nichols Field in Manila and Clark field about 50 miles north of Manila.

Manila had been declared an open city, but despite that fact there had been a great deal of damage done, including the burning of all the big oil installations by the time the Japanese entered the doomed city, the "Pearl of the Orient", on January 1, 1942. Late Christmas afternoon some of the men came up the hill with the disturbing news that we were to be evacuated the following morning at eight o'clock. There was hasty packing of the few possessions we had brought with us, and a hurried trip into town to get a few more things essential to even a minimum of comfort, for we well knew that we would never be able to obtain anything once the enemy took possession of the city. We were determined to have decent beds and when the cavalcade left for our new destination, every car had mattresses piled on top. The order was not for compulsory evacuation, but we were all willing to go for the sake of greater safety, especially for the children. Late that afternoon we arrived at the big sugar central, which was to house us for the next few weeks. The men went down to the city from time to time, but there was no business done for there was no communications possible. We had had no mail since the taking of Manila, and one ship, the Corregidor, attempting to return to Cebu was sunk and hundreds of people drowned. As the days and weeks rolled on we felt we could not go on indefinitely in the Central crowded where 45 were housed under one roof. We had yet to learn what real crowding was. Finally, our men got together a crew of Filipino workmen and materials to construct a new camp for us. The buildings were of bamboo and matting, but were new and clean, and we settled down with considerable comfort and a fair amount of privacy. We had a Delco plant to generate power for light and refrigeration. We organized the children into a sort of school routine, assigned various tasks in the kitchen department, and began a new life. *Here appears a hand written notation "Black outs".*

Every day the bombers circled over our heads, but no attack was made on the town. We had plenty of food for several ships from Australia destined for Bataan never got any further than Cebu and we had free access to their cargos. We could have faced this life indefinitely with a fair degree of equanimity, but we knew it could not last. We felt sure the Japs would come as soon as Bataan fell. On April 6 came the fateful news. Bataan had fallen and the Death March had begun. No one will ever know how many thousands perished on the way to Cabanatuan, as the starving, wounded men made their way to camp Connell, perhaps 25,000 would be a conservative guess.

The people of Cebu had no intention of declaring it an open city and letting the Japs come in and find it a going concern, as they had taken Manila. For weeks our Signal Corps had been busy mining all the streets of the business section and their approaches. On the morning of April 9th the Japs landed about 14 km south of the city. The demolition squad went to work and soon nothing of the downtown area was left but a mass of tangled wire and rubble. The bridges were all blown up, and the greater part of the remaining civilian population left on foot for another camp in the hills, among them my daughter. A few foreigners assembled in the home of the British Vice Consul to await developments.

The electric light plant had been bombed, the water mains were broken by the explosion of the mines, so, all in all, the Japs found little that was of any use to them. They were now in the driver's seat. On the outbreak we had interned all the Japs and Germans and now it was their turn to intern us. On April 30 came our orders to report to the city the following morning.

Another hasty packing and we were on our way to God only knew where. The bridges were all out, our own doing to be sure, but fortunately it was the dry season, and with the aid of caribou and ropes, the cars all got across the beds of the streams, all except one, on which were some of my possessions, among them all of my flat silver which I had made sure of taking with me when we left Cebu. I may mention that five years afterwards it was returned to be through the good offices of President Osmena's daughter-in-law. She had rescued it from the guerillas and buried it on her own property. When she became suspected of a friendly attitude toward the Americans, Gen. McArthur sent a P.T. boat to take her to Leyte, and she turned the silver over to Capt. Messa, a Spaniard, and from him it came back to me in L.A. in 1947.

On arrival in Cebu we were installed in the home of the manager of the Chartered Bank where we stayed until the next day, when we were transferred to the Provincial jail. My presence there was not without irony, as my friends reminded me of the hundreds of offenders my husband had sent there in the course of the 25 years he had been Judge of the District. The place was filthy, although some of our men had been sent over to make some pretense of cleaning it. Hercules had hardly a worse job with the Augean stables. We were introduced to the Japanese routine by which we were always landed in a new place just before nightfall, when it was difficult to establish ourselves. Perhaps that was their idea of psychological warfare. I wish I could tell you what the army of occupation looked like. They might have been animals walking on two instead of four legs. Many of them had two and three wristwatches, and Parker 51 pens bristled from their pockets. At sundown bayonets were fixed to the ends of their rifles.

There were no stoves in the jail, but our men with the inventiveness which never deserted them in all the dreary years to come soon had fixed up substitutes from broken lengths of cement piping, with holes for draft and bars from the jail windows for grids to hold cooking utensils. We still had plenty of food, although we had been obliged to leave thousands of pesos worth of commissaries in our first camp. The courtyard of the jail was all of concrete, and soon the children were playing Hop Scotch, and first thing we knew, one of the guards was hopping about with them. I remember we had canned baked-beans, and for dessert, *something* Australian.

The night was pretty terrible. The quarters were alive with vermin and the beds made of narrow slats of wood with half-inch spaces between offered ideal accommodation for them. Next morning the courtyard was a scene of intense activity, everyone had his bed out and was pouring boiling water and crinoline over it. We were fortunate that there were some few bottles of disinfectant in the so-called hospital. The population of bed bugs was cut into but never exterminated. Perhaps you can imagine what it would be like to sleep at cot-level, or on the floor with 15-foot walls around you, and the few small windows ten feet above you which never seemed to admit a breath of fresh air. All this in the midst of the hot season.

I was among the more fortunate very small minority who were assigned to space above what had been the jail hospital. One of the American women had three children, the youngest about 18 months old. Every hour a sentry would come clumping up the stairs into the room where we were and turn his flashlight on every bed to see that no one was missing. Where he thought anyone could go in the middle of the night from behind stone walls and barbed wire, I wouldn't know. The sound of their scuffing feet in what was probably the first pair of shoes and the thumping of their bayonets on the stone stairs left a lasting memory. One night the mother of the little 18-month old girl was almost beside herself hearing the constant crying of her little one, and had pulled her bed to the top of the stairs to catch any possible breath of air. But it was of no use. We had done all we could for her and finally gave up in the hope that she might cry herself to sleep. Suddenly we heard the clump, clump of the sentry's boots and his bayonet. It was a bright moonlight night, and we could see him standing by the baby's bed and lifting the mosquito net. We were paralyzed with fear, but dared not say a word. We were amazed at hearing him say, "No papa, no Mama, No cry. Hmmmm." He put the net down and off down the stairs he shuffled. The little girl is now a High School student, living in Laguna Beach with her mother.

After two weeks we were transferred to the Cebu Junior College in which I was a faculty member. This move was not ordered because of any consideration for us, but because the Japs wanted the jail for the military prisoners who were soon to arrive.

On the tenth of May they brought in the other civilian prisoners, among them my daughter. On the 6th of May had come the expected news of the fall of Corregidor, the bombing of which was on a par with that of Gibraltar. A few days later the first of the military prisoners arrived, but we were forbidden to speak to them, although among them we saw many of our next-door neighbors, men who had volunteered for service after Pearl Harbor. At the end of the week we were sent to our new camp at the College and we never saw one of them again. They were all lost on one of the bombed ships after surviving Bilibid, Cabanatuan and Davao prisons. The ships on which they were traveling carried no distinguishing marks or lights and were bombed by our own men in the belief that they were enemy craft.

My daughter, married to a Britisher, had registered British in the event that her husband should survive the war and was interned in a schoolhouse a few hundred yards from the College. From Dec. 22 until 14 of the following June she did not know whether he was dead or alive. On the latter date he appeared at the British camp, looking like someone from the grave, en route to England, thinking that her orders would have arrived for her to accompany him. But no orders had come, and after about five minutes he had to leave without her. Three days later the orders came and the Jap interpreter took her out to the airport for the trip to Manila. From there after a delay of six weeks they went on to Shanghai to await the arrival of other consular groups. A Japanese ship took them to Portuguese East Africa where they were transferred to an Egyptian ship for England. I didn't see her again for four years.

The Junior College offered little more in the way of conveniences than the jail, but there was more room as we had the out-doors to live in and our men had soon displayed their ability to make something out of nothing. Stoves were contrived from cement pipes, showers were rigged from petroleum tins and the men hauled the water from a near-by well. Among the internees were about a dozen members of a Norwegian ship that was bombed on the first day of the war. Peter, the chief cook, was a godsend, as was Nels, the chief electrician, who managed to find enough tangled wire to string a few lights through the building. The Japanese gave us not one cent, and those of us who had money simply carried those who had none. Many of the dependents were old beachcombers who had been in the islands ever since the Spanish-American War, living out in the hills with their native wives and families.

In the evening we would occasionally play bridge under a 40-candle power electric bulb, with the curious Japanese sentries leaning over our chairs and breathing down our necks. Since the only American doctor in Cebu had been quarantined, who was one of the first to be taken prisoner, we had no medical personnel in the camp. A Filipino doctor was allowed in on one or two occasions when help was absolutely necessary.

The sentries were supposed to wear boots, but one decided to go back to his soft shoes. One night he came into the dormitory when everyone was in bed, took up his position at the foot of a very lovely young woman, part Indian. As she lay there asleep he stood staring at her until one of the other women happened to stir and saw him. She let out a yell, and he disappeared. We reported it to the committee the next morning. The interpreter was warned if anything should happen again, it would be taken up with high command, for guards had been warned by their superiors that they were not to molest the internees. He evidently was reprimanded by the interpreter for he didn't wear the soft shoes any more, and what is more, we never had hourly visits to the dormitories. But he tried to take it out on us in other ways. The next afternoon when he went on duty he made one of our women sweep the floor of the upstairs balcony three times. A few minutes later, as I sat out on the front portico of the college, he was standing beside one of the pillars. He saw a cigarette stub lying on one of the steps and motioned to me to come and pick it up. I shook my head and indicated he might do it. Again, he told me to do it and I paid no attention to him but went on reading. I had made up my mind I wouldn't do it unless he absolutely forced me to. I could almost feel the back of my neck tighten up and two of our committee men who were also on the porch sat there fearful of what the little creature might do. But, after a moment, he leaned over and kicked the cigarette away.

The Junior College was pretty well out of town and we had plenty of room both in the building and in the grounds surrounding it. A barbed wire fence marked the out-of-bounds. We ate out of doors, a pleasant enough arrangement at the time of year. A detail of our men got breakfast, Pete looked after lunch, and two of the women cooked the dinner with three or four men tending the fires, no small job since we had no stoves except the ones improvised by the men and most of the wood was green. One never knows what he can do until the time comes. We made biscuits, gingerbread and corn bread, baking them in native ovens with a fire on top as well as under the oven. The best things and those in the smallest quantities were kept for the children. When anyone would cast a longing eye at a can of tomato juice or canned fruit, he would be warned, "You can't have that, that is for the little darlings."

The middle of October arrived and we were moved again, this time to the Filipino Club nearer town. The guerillas had been coming down almost to the barbed wire fence surrounding the College, and on more than one occasion shots were exchanged between them and the sentries.

(Editor's note: _The American Guerillas In The Philippines_ by Ira Wolfert, New York: Simon and Schuster published in 1945 depicts the efforts of those fierce troops who fought the Japanese during the occupation. Great Grandmother Claire knew most of the characters in the book personally. It is well worth the read. I have copies to borrow.)

Before we left the interpreter saw me prowling around in the library looking for some books to take with us for the children's schoolwork. He glowered at me and said, "No books." I made no reply but I got some of the men to collect some old wet rice sacks, which we filled and tossed on the truck just as it was leaving the grounds. Three years later I had the pleasure of returning to the university in Manila about a thousand pesos worth of books, which we managed to take with us.

When we moved to the Filipino Club the British internees joined us so we had 120 in camp. We found about the same inconveniences but we had gotten used to them and our men, as usual, soon overcame the worst of them. The Japanese never could understand how the Americans could laugh and joke and have fun. They were such a browbeaten lot when we interned them, they thought they would find us the same when our turn came. Halloween we had a party with all the nonsense that one would expect, and the guards stood around open-mouthed with wonder and amusement. The guerillas could have walked right into camp, so intent were our captors on the show.

One day the commandant came to the camp accompanied by a newspaperman and an interpreter. Two of our committee went to the gate to meet them. In the course of conversation, translated word for word, the reporter asked, "Who will win the war?" One of the Americans answered, "The Americans will win." Whereupon the interpreter solemnly passed the answer on to the reporter, who just as solemnly wrote, "The Americans will win the war." Some of the Japanese visitors could speak considerable English and one of them asked one of our boys, "What are you Americans, are you all optimists or are you just nuts? "Just nuts." was the answer.

Thanksgiving Day many of the Filipinos came to the gate bringing us all kinds of food and the guards looked on with greedy eyes as we sailed into it. Quantities of warm clothing accompanied the food, for in some way the rumor had arisen that we were to be sent to Formosa.

On Dec 31st we entered the worst phase of our internment. We were loaded on a filthy troop ship, which had been down to the East Indies carrying soldiers. Four of our number were very ill and were allowed to sleep up on the hatchways in the open air but with no protection against the hot sun by day or the rains that came on at night. The rest of us were put a deck below, ankle-deep with bilge water, which we tried to blot up with great piles of newspapers brought with us from Junior College. It was certainly a comedown for the "Manchester Guardian" and the "New York Times". We begged the ship's officers to allow the sick people to sleep in some vacant cabins, which we could see. But it was useless. The trip took six days and nights and should have been made in 36 hours. At Iloilo we took on 165 Filipino prisoners. We were shut up in the lower hold until they were all aboard for fear we might exchange even a look of sympathy or understanding with them. On the whole packed ship there were no sanitary provisions, only a long trough running along the side of each deck which was flushed out two or three times a day. Shutters about three feet in height were the only attempt at privacy and it was really amusing to see some man carefully guarding and holding the door while some woman occupied the space behind it. Modesty was at a discount.

On January 19 we arrived at Santo Tomas, the Manila camp which already held about 6,000 (Note: This number is not accurate; closer to 4000-mbk) internees. It is one of the oldest and largest universities in Manila and was giving degrees when the Pilgrims landed on Plymouth Rock. The classrooms and all the laboratories had been turned into dormitories, each with anywhere from 40 to 709 occupants.

This was our first Christmas in camp and it was amazing to see what had been done to make it a happy day for the children. The men had made toys and the women had dressed dolls. The committee gave us a very decent dinner. I didn't go into the main camp for a week, but into a little camp hospital suffering from a bad case of double-distilled hate, which manifested itself in a very sore throat. I had been in the dormitory a week when good luck came my way. At the College of the Holy Ghost was an annex to which the Japs sent the overflow of small children. Some of my good Catholic friends asked that I be sent to join them there and on Jan 6th I left the congested area of Santa Tomas for the much more pleasant surroundings of the College. The Filipino doctor who had been in charge was relieved for other duty and an American registered nurse took her place.

The convent had been occupied by the Americans as a hospital and much of the equipment was left behind. We had a staff of about 30 and some household help, a Chinese cook and a Filipino lavandera. We of the staff had to do everything for ourselves. Once a week I went down town shopping. A red armband proclaimed the fact that I was out with permission and I never encountered any unpleasantness. There were still fairly ample food supplies in Manila if one had the money to buy them, for prices kept mounting. After 7 o'clock in the evening we could use the kitchen for our own bits of cooking and we had many a good meal of pork chops and other substantial items of food. We made our own coco honey and peanut butter. We had no Japanese sentries and no roll-call, and when I went into town I took precious good care to walk on the other side of the street from where the sentry was posted, and thereby avoided the necessity of bowing to him. Failure to observe this formality could bring a sharp rap of the sentry's rifle butt, or at best, a slap in the face.

And so, thirteen months rolled by. Our surroundings were more than pleasant in the spacious tree-shaded convent grounds, and there were five American Sisters, only two of whom were associated with us at first. Later, two more joined the staff. One of them was so tall and commanding in appearance we called her the "Roman Senator". I have sense enough to know when I am even comparatively well off and to the 13 months I spent at Holy Ghost College I attribute much of the unbroken health I enjoyed throughout the war. But it was all too good to last.

By February 1944 the Japs could see the writing on the wall, and with the consolidation of the outside camps we were returned to Santa Tomas. The idea simply appalled me. The thought of going into one of the overcrowded dormitories, with the ocean of mosquito nets, brought to my mind the feeling of suffocation that would overtake me for I knew that last comers always got the locations farthest from the windows. However, my fears were not realized for a vacancy occurred in the dormitory where several of my Cebu friends were assigned, and I got a place near a window.

Christmas 1942 we had all received Red Cross boxes and we still were spinning them out 15 months later. The food supply was growing noticeably less. Many of the internees were beginning to show the effects of their confinement, which had already lasted two years and a half. There were children in camp who had come in as babies and could remember no other life. To them, the only way to have food served was to stand in endless lines waiting for it to be dished up from the huge "kauas", big black iron pans about three feet across and a foot or more deep. One day the little girl who had been a baby in the provincial jail now approaching four was telling some of the still smaller children the story of "The Three Bears". "And when Goldilocks went into the house of the three bears she saw three dishes of mush on the table. And they were big dishes for Papa Bear had been through the line twice". Some of the children's fathers lived in the Education Building and one little fellow asked his father, "Daddy, when I get to be a big man do you think I can live in the Education Building with you?" Horrible thought.

The Japanese had opened another camp about 45 miles from Manila and several hundred internees had been sent there. Several of my friends were to go in the next contingent after my arrival in Santo Tomas, and they made it possible for me to join them. Again my luck held. Los Banos was on the site of the Agricultural College of the University of the Philippines and besides the permanent college buildings and the homes of the faculty there were 28 barracks, which had been built for the Filipino soldiers. These were of native materials but quite new and clean. Each contained 48 cubicles, large enough for two single beds and a bit of other furniture such as a small dressing table if anyone happened to possess one. Families could be together and there was a semblance of privacy that had been sorely lacking at Santo Tomas. There was a central hall and a crosswalk halfway down, and between every two barracks a bathhouse in which the supply of water varied from never very much to hardly any. Wide eaves overhanging the outside walls gave shade and beyond those were little thatched shacks where we could cook, when we had anything to cook. For a while we had a small canteen where we could buy a few things like bananas, papayas and native coffee. Occasionally there would be an opportunity to buy a few pounds of sugar, which we called "muscovado", raw sugar that had been dried on the open ground and through which goats and bare-footed natives had walked at will. But we were not fussy, sugar was energy.

There were the same old chow lines but not much at the end of them. Every morning a group of women would be assigned to clean the rice for the corn meal for the day's meal, and I mean "meal", for by now we were down to one a day consisting of a plate of rotten cornmeal, or on very rare occasions, a plate of third class rice. The Filipinos had learned it was no use for them to try to raise anything for us for the Japanese appropriated everything. So large numbers took their families and their caribous and went to the hills where they would plant a little corn and a few camotes (sweet potatoes) and managed to exist. They dared not try to help us. Punishment was swift and sure. One Filipino who had given a cigarette to an American was given the water cure by which a man's body is filled with water poured into his mouth from a hose until it is fearfully bloated and then he is beaten unmercifully with the same hose.

The lack of all fresh vegetables began to show in the cases of beriberi. The women, and the men too, would follow the dry bed of some little stream and pick handfuls of pigweed, strip the burrs from the stem and put the leaves in the rice. One of the men was a few feet outside the fence doing this when a Jap guard saw him and shot and killed him. A young Pan American pilot met the same fate as he was crawling back into the camp. His head and shoulders were already on the camp side when the sentry shot him. The boy begged for a priest when he knew he was dying and, although there were at least 25 priests in the barracks not more than a hundred feet away, the guard refused to call one and the boy lay there and bled to death. There were no coffins and the body was simply wrapped in a straw mat and put into a shallow grave.

Our hospital was now filled with cases of beriberi and there was little medicine to supply the vitamin lack, which is so largely responsible for the disease. We had a fine doctor from Shanghai who had been caught in Manila, as had so many others. Eleven Navy nurses whose plane had gone down over Lake Lanao completed the staff, and a fine staff it was. The caliber of the internees at Los Banos was, with a very few exceptions, well above the average. Among the outstanding people were the heads of the National Bank in Manila and the English Chartered Bank, Bishop Binstead of the Episcopal Church in Japan, a fine group of Catholic priests and nuns, and a man known throughout Asia, Donald of Chins, on whose head the Japanese had placed a price, and who never even bothered to change his name, but lived right under the eyes of the people who would have boiled him in oil if they could have caught him. One of the radio broadcasters from Manila was another internee whose name was Clarence Belial. As Don Bell, he was an anathema to the Japs. His pre-war broadcasts had been devastating to the Japs but they never knew that he was right in their midst. They even assigned to him the duty of making all the official announcements of the camp over the loud speaker. Later, during the tests at Bikini, we heard his unmistakable voice as he broadcast the news from one of the battle-ships.

One of the barracks was set aside for school on weekdays and church services on Sunday. Another was given the Catholics for their exclusive use. There was nothing in the way of equipment for the schoolwork but a few blackboards, but with the crude accommodations, a large group of children went on with their studies and lost not a day in their standings when they returned to school in the States. The adult population profited as well for there were many accomplished teachers in advanced subjects. Such activities were a wonderful aid in keeping up the morale of the camp and many people knew a lot more when they came out than when they went in.

At this time we, of course, had nothing in the way of news, only rumors, and DID we have rumors. It was generally felt that the end could not be too far off but whether we would be there to see it was a moot question and the thought of what might happen to internees in remote camps was not a pleasant one. After Gen. McArthur landed in Leyte in October 1944 the Japs made practically no attempt to feed us. Beriberi was increasing and most of the time the cornmeal mush had to be eaten without coconut milk or sugar, sometimes it was even cooked without salt. When our committee made demands for more food the Japs would say they would be glad to give it to us if they had it, but we must remember that their own men were starving out in the field. All we thought was that we would like to be starving the way they were and not the way we were. We could not even get what were called "mongo beans", a kind of cowpea, which would have been a great help in staving off the inroads of beriberi.

Christmas came, the fourth under Japanese control. There was very little in the way of celebration for there was nothing to celebrate with. The Catholic Church held the mid-night service on Christmas Eve, the Noche Burna. Somehow we didn't notice the dirty bamboo framework, the earthen floor and the hard wooden benches. The dignity and beauty of the service and the lovely music were enough. And anyway, there was no glamour in the settings of the first Christmas scene.

After the holidays the school classes were not resumed. The Japs forbade anyone's being away from his barracks except in the performance of camp duties. The bombing grew heavier and heavier and we felt there was literally something in the air. Three or four of our men had gone over the fence to get to McArthur's lines with the word that people were dying of starvation and beriberi. Strangely enough, there were no reprisals. In the hills back of us the guerillas under Col. Ramsay were very active and our men had joined up with them, though we did not know that until long after. In the early morning of Jan 7th there was wild commotion in the camp. The Japanese garrison hastily abandoned the camp, even leaving in the middle of a meal with food still cooking on the stoves. They had simply turned the camp over to the committee and left. Cries of "We are free" ran through the camp and at seven o'clock we all went up to the administration building and the Stars and Stripes rose slowly to the top of the flag pole and we heard again the familiar songs that had been forbidden for so long, the "Star Spangled Banner" and "God Bless America".

We had one week of freedom and then, early in the morning the patrol went through the barracks calling out "Important announcement!

Important announcement! The commandant and his staff are back. Keep away from all sentry boxes." During the week of their absence the Filipinos had poured into camp bring us sugar, bananas and some rice, all taken from their own scanty stores in the hills. We wanted to pay them but they would accept only such things as we could find to give in exchange.

We learned later that the commandant thought that McArthur was landing at Batangas, not very far south of us, and he decided it would be a good idea to pull out in the opposite direction. Instead, he was landing at San Fernando Union, 120 miles north of Manila, and we gathered that our contingent had been pretty well slapped down by the high command. At any rate, they were back.

Their false move didn't improve their already ugly tempers and we were given still less food. A plate of rotten corn meal at 9:30 every morning constituted our daily ration. There were some go-betweens in the camp and I gave one of them a $100 diamond solitaire for about ten pounds of rice and ten pounds of sugar. Two days after I got it half of it was stolen. All I could think was that whomever took it must have been more hungry than I.

Every day the bombing grew heavier and there was no resistance on the part of the Japs. On Washington's Birthday it was so heavy the ground shook under our feet. At five minutes to seven on the morning of the 23rd of February, a bomber passed in front of the camp, and when it was just in front of us a banner was let over the side with "Rescue" on it. We could hardly believe our eyes and dared make no sign that we had seen it for we had been forbidden to look up as planes passed and disobedience would be a serious matter. A Seventh Day Adventist minister received a rifle butt in his jaw for failure to obey the order. I rather think he felt it was worth it. In just five minutes nine bombers came over the lake near which our camp was situated and the paratroopers began to drop, 100 or more of the 11th Airborne, rushed the camp and killed the garrison of about 110. We learned later how the operation was so successful. The Japanese are fanatical on the subject of physical exercise and our men had reported that every morning at seven o'clock they were in the barracks for setting up exercises and had not their side arms on.

As the paratroopers began firing the guerillas in the hills just back of us started a fusillade. We were between the two lines of fire but we gave no thought to that and only a couple of people were hit, and not badly injured.

Our paratroopers went into each of the barracks to order the occupants to get ready for evacuation immediately, that they only had five hours to clear the camp, that 8,000 Japs would be in by six o'clock and it would take two trips to do it. They were still in control of the highway between where we were and Manila and 59 amphibian tanks, "am tracks", were to carry us to Muntinglupa where the 21st Evacuation Hospital had been set up only a week before. As the troopers in the cross walk in my barracks spoke, a little woman came from one of the cubicles dragging a small trunk. He asked her what that was. She said, "That is my trunk with my things in it". He said, "You can't take with you" and she replied," I cannot go and leave all my belongings". His answer settled it. "Alright lady, stay and burn with them. We are setting fire to these barracks in five minutes". I said, "What about luggage?' He said, "No luggage unless you are already packed." I had an over-night case with some papers in it which I had always had ready in case of fire of typhoon.

People came streaming out of the barracks with what possessions they could grab up at a moment's notice. A few had suitcases but most of them had pillowcases stuffed with the most essential things. I myself had no time to get a Chinese chest out from under my bed, and started my return home in a skirt made of an old window curtain and a man's T-shirt. I did have one cotton dress hanging up in the cubicle, and that was the one in which I landed in San Pedro three months later.

As the more than two thousand internees gathered in the open spaces, the flame- throwers were applied to all the buildings and in a few minutes the 28 barracks were a seething mass of flames. The troopers told us that when the mission was initiated the commanding officer told his men that he could promise nothing in the way of success, that it meant going 25 miles behind the enemy's lines, but it must be attempted. He asked for volunteers and every one of the 450 men stood up. Not wanting to choose from the volunteers, he had them draw lots. The commanding officers of the troopers said to me, 'This will probably appear in the States papers as just another mission but to us it is the biggest thing we have done in the War. We would not have believed it possible to take out over 2000 people of every age and temperament without one single case of panic or obstruction, but it has been 100% successful".

When the Amtracks had lined up the first five were filled with hospital cases, many of whom would not have lived another 48 hours. We had people in my Amtrak who were shot by Jap snipers who were hiding in the little islands in the lake, one of them seriously, but who recovered. About noon we reached Muntinglupa, and had our first meal, not much of a meal either for we had been on starvation diet so long that we were given food only in small quantities for the first week, and the doctors in the hospital superintended the issuing of all rations. That noon we had only a plate of pea soup and three crackers. For six weeks we remained at Muntinglupa while we were getting back to normal and while the arrangements were being made for our transportation home.

During our stay we were allowed to go down to Santo Tomas where we got the story of the release of that camp by the 1st Cavalry, and of the terrible days that followed it. The Japanese, with their backs against the wall, began an orgy of slaughter. Mr. Carol Grinnell, Eastern representative of General Electric and Mr. Duggleby, one of the heads of Benguet Consolidated Mines were beheaded, their bodies cut in two and buried in a shallow trench where they were found by the Americans. The same fate overtook an old friend of mine from Zamboanga. She had a son in the Army and the Japs chose to think she knew where he was and could give them some information about him and his companions. As a matter of fact, she knew no more about them than we did. But she was put in the dungeons at the old Fort Santiago in Manila and tortured until her mind gave way and was finally executed, as were ten others of my old friends in Manila who were bayoneted and beheaded at their own table, only because they had white faces. Santo Tomas had its own story, which was more tragic than ours, but to us it all seems one because we had shared many of the earlier days of internment with them. It was only later that we learned that the Los Banos camp had been marked for annihilation on the morning the troopers came. The plan was to line us all up for inspection then rake the lines with machine guns.

On April 9th, the third anniversary of the occupation of Cebu, we were taken in Army trucks to Manila to start our trip home. We saw the awful devastation on every side, the worst of any in the war with the exception of Warsaw. The lovely, picturesque old Walled City was in ruins, and my last view left me with no desire ever to see it again. People going out now for the first time find much that is pleasant and even charming, but to me, there would always be the memory of the city as I had known it for over 40 years.

Our trip home on the ADMIRAL EBERLE was pretty grim in some ways but no one complained, we were headed for the United States. We had no convoy, only two destroyers, one port side and one on the starboard. We had to travel without lights for there still were Jap subs floating around and the war did not come to an end for another four months. There were no port holes for the ship was supposed to be air conditioned, but the internment had been relieved on such short notice that there was insufficient shipping to bring them all home immediately. In my cabin were 18 berths with 24 people sleeping in them, the extra six were children who had to sleep with their mothers. No one was allowed on deck after dusk and it was a real hardship to go below into the unventilated cabins, but the captain would not risk panic in case of alarm. I never saw the sun sinking below the horizon that I don't recall the M.P. going along the deck, swinging his stick and calling, "All passengers lay below. Ladies forward, gentlemen aft, Marines and garbage over the side".

The one stop we made after leaving Manila was for 36 hours at Ulithe, the point from which the attack on Okinawa was launched. Just outside Honolulu we lay to while a dozen F.B.I. men came aboard to screen the passengers. One of them said to me one day, "When you get home, don't bother telling people in general about all that you have gone through. They will be mildly interested, but they will begin to tell you how they couldn't buy cigarettes and how their meat was rationed." I am glad to say that I found that attitude very rare. Perhaps one cannot realize pain if he has never felt pain, and I believe the people did everything they could to help the cause, and after all, money was terribly important and they gave that in full measure.

On May 2nd we arrived in San Pedro. The plan had been for us to land in San Francisco but it was the week of the United Nations and the hotels sent word that they could not undertake to accommodate the number arriving. We were taken to the Elks Club in Los Angeles where everything possible was done for our comfort. Within a few hours we had all been assigned to hotels unless friends or relatives were within call. Later, transportation was arranged and on the 6th of May I reached San Francisco after an absence of exactly seven years.

I cannot close this not-altogether pleasant account without a tribute to the Filipino people for their almost entire loyalty to the Americans. They risked their lives in many cases to help us. When they were in great need themselves they never availed themselves of the temptation to sell out an American they knew to be in hiding in their neighborhood. For what they did for us they asked and expected nothing in return. One man in Cebu, Don Ramon Aboitiz, made himself responsible for thousands of pesos, which were advanced us through the years, and when he came to Los Angeles in 1948 and I, along with some of the other Cebuano's tried to repay some of the money, which we had received in camp, he refused to accept a cent. He just smiled and said, "You don't owe me anything. No one owes me anything". In contrast to this, I may mention that a note I had given for a hundred dollars to the General Electric Co. manager was promptly collected by the main office in New York as soon as I was known to have arrived in the States.

Conditions have changed throughout the Orient. A new feeling of intense nationalism prevails everywhere, and anyone not a Filipino is an alien. I would not care to return to live in a country where my flag had been at the top of the pole to see another one there. And yet, I should like to think that many of my old friends would still be friends, whatever their politics.

We hope that the infiltration of Communism may be counteracted by the present government, which still has a great deal to learn. Gov. Taft's promissory note of eventual independence came due in 1946 and in its new roll the government has to fight the evils present there as everywhere corruption and graft. To this is added the natural antagonism between the prevailing political parties. But there is a good man at the head, Ramon Magsaysay, a man of the people, and if he can only get a fair amount of the cooperation, the future offers some promise. Economic conditions are far from satisfactory and money control is very rigid.

It should never be forgotten that the Filipinos are the only Christian nation in the Orient and they constitute a bulwark for us in the fight against the forces that would destroy our Western world. Their faith in the United States is largely the corner stone of their own attempt at building up a democratic form of government, and it is the wish of every one who has their interests at heart, that we do not let them down.

And so, "Mabuhay", which, like "Aloha" can mean anything one wants it to mean."

Printed in the United States
By Bookmasters